Baqubah:

Bones and Blood

Aaron Lee Marshall

With a Forward by Lieutenant Colonel **David Pearson**

And an introduction by **Matt Harlock**

Edited by **Christopher Hislop** and **Laura Marshall**

baqubah press - barrington new hampshire - 2020

ISBN 978-1-79485-080-4 (paperback)

THIS BOOK IS DEDICATED TO

Alan J. Burgess K.I.A. October 15, 2004 on patrol in Mosul, Iraq. Turret Gunner, Father, Brother, and Son.

Some words about Baqubah: Bones and Blood

"Fight Club meets Black Hawk Down. Baqubah hits you in the face with warrior grit that only a soldier fully understands. War is rough. Our Armed Forces come home with a language that at times is painful to listen to but keeps your attention in awe. Humbled, honored and thankful to read these stories about the men who protect our freedom."
Tim Brigham *Founder and President of The Superhero Collective*

"We live strange."
Dave Emeney, Musician

"This book depicts exactly how we lived, how we felt, and what we thought on an everyday basis. Aaron hit it perfectly."
SSG. Michael J. Ramsey Retired (Veteran of Baqubah 04-05)

"After 15 years of being discharged from the Army, this book is filled with brutally raw stories that brought me back to a place I had once tried to forget. I have chosen to take my experiences from Iraq to give me perspective of how fortunate I am to be an American, a husband and a father. I am glad to see that Marshall's focus is to help others cope with the aftermath of war as there needs to be more public awareness of what many deals with after they take off the uniform."

SPC. Tim Siefken (Veteran of Baqubah 04-05)

"I hope you put the time we were filling sandbags after April 9th, and you stole my chicken cavatelli MRE. If it's not, put it in the movie please; it was historical."

SPC Jameson Holmes (Veteran of Baqubah 04-05)

"Raw. Honest. And informative. Aaron's account of war and his life after returning paints a picture of overcoming mental and physical evils. To learn
"This book is so intense, it's not for a single sitting or an hour reading. It needs to be taken in small pieces, lived with and let go. Hell isn't a place one wants to linger."

Jeanne' McCartin, NH Arts & Entertainment Writer

about the domestic and foreign tragedies of war from firsthand accounts cannot easily be consumed but is more palatable with the use of juxtaposition that Aaron provides. My hope for this book is that it is read by people for generations to come, as the profound importance it provides is something that simply cannot be unraveled. Baqubah: Bones and Blood is at times chilling but proves that the human spirit is often found in the least likely of places."

Austin Mills, Director of Media for the Dam Media Company

"The things that bothered me the most was knowing I had friends who were killed; being behind Norbie and Dawn's Humvee and not having a target to shoot at. I felt helpless. It bothered me seeing innocent people laying in the streets dismembered, seeing a six-year-old boy's skull and blood in the back seat of a car, his body covered on the ground and his father and younger brother having to drive that same car away from the checkpoint. I have no regrets about killing the enemy."

Darren "Moose" Ripley (Veteran of Baqubah 04-05)

"Awesome read. Highly recommend to anyone that was in or around the military."

Chad Ralph PVT USMC MWSS-171 Iwakuni, Japan

"Raw, so very real and amazingly awe-inspiring. Aaron writes as if you are sitting across from him engaging in a candid conversation. You can genuinely see how his brain is processing his observations and can honestly imagine some of the emotions he experienced. The fact that this fascinating memoir is written to support the true heroes of our country process unimaginable trauma experiences is beyond touching. As a social worker with a significant trauma informed recovery-based practice, I will use the experiences from this book and knowledge and insight I gained from reading it to better support people in need. PTSD is something that requires appropriate resources, understanding and support NOW. "Why not arm them with the knowledge that it takes to keep them alive AFTER war?' I could not put the book down and highly recommend it!"

Shawna Chase, Program Administrator *Tri-County Mental Health*

"Aaron accurately describes the way it was in Baqubah. The day the Kiowa was shot down and the hell of fire that erupted was one of the times that I will never forget. April 9th, 2004, the day that will haunt many for life is etched there as well. I am proud of my brother Aaron and his completion of his book Baqubah: Bones and Blood."

Sgt. Ryan Trahan (Veteran of Baqubah '04)

"Baqubah: Bones and Blood was very eye opening and taught me a lot of things I couldn't have even imagined let alone experienced!"

Larry Warren - Carpenter (Boston local 327)

"Marshall reminds me of Medal of Honor Recipient Maynard Smith, who demonstrated exceptional bravery under fire, but always found trouble when the bullets were not flying. Still he was someone I wanted by my side when the shooting started."

CSM Christopher St. Cyr (Veteran of Baqubah 04-05)

Foreword

Baqubah: Bones and Blood offers the perspective from one young soldier about an obscure New Hampshire Army National Guard artillery unit sent to Iraq at the beginning of the burgeoning, soon to turn hyper-violent, insurgency. These soldiers, skilled in the field artillery mission of firing 155mm M197 towed howitzers at targets miles away, were repackaged, in the words of the Army, for a new mission: "In Lieu Of" military police. Knowing nothing of the Military Police (MP) mission and with no training specific to that specialty, this unit, repackaged as the 197th MP Company, was sent off to Iraq for Operation Iraqi Freedom II to "mop up" after the initial invasion, or so they thought.

Aaron Lee Marshall tells the graphic, deeply personal story, about how a person rises to an incredible challenge, survives, and deals with the aftermath of getting coldcocked by physical and psychological horrors, visual scenes that defy the surreal, and a vibe that would fit in better with a movie like *Apocalypse Now* or *Platoon*.

The mission and the mobilization preparation at Ft Dix, New Jersey in January of 2004 focused on individual soldier skills like weapons qualification and first aid, rather than the more complex art of training collectively for urban counterinsurgency operations as an MP unit acting as a team at the Army squad and platoon level.

Nobody expected what was about to happen next.

The 197th MP Company was built up from soldiers assigned mostly to the 2nd Battalion, 197th Field Artillery of the NH ARNG. Of the roughly 300 or so soldiers in this battalion, about 175 mobilized to Iraq as MPs. As senior army leaders determined strategic plans for Iraq in what is referred to as stability operations – which is what an Army does once it secures an objective – in this case, Iraq, they realized we had army units such as the 2/197 FA that had soldiers who could do a lot of things, but had no mission.

There was little use for artillery units once coalition forces had secured Iraq and toppled the government. Units such as these could be repurposed quickly to do other missions such as basic security and other low intensity tasks that didn't require a lot of training. And with this "field-expedient" concept in place the 197th MP Company was called up and mobilized to go to Iraq "In Lieu Of" actually trained MPs to be turned over to local commanders in Iraq to perform whatever tasks needed to be accomplished in a roughly secure environment.

With great enthusiasm, and some great and talented skill sets from civilian careers, the 197th, like the rest of coalition ground forces and our military and civilian leaders walked into a wild west of insurgent and terrorist violence that we never imagined possible...

These soldiers went off expecting a relatively uneventful tour of duty, wondering if they would see any action at all, and getting as much as just about any unit in the Iraq War. One can look to the lack of preparation and training, the In Lieu Of mission that was outside the norm, the change in doctrinal thinking that hobbled the unit's leaders from making better plans for the mission and better preparing the soldiers for the mission and say it was an unfortunate circumstance for all involved, and everyone who came home could use available benefits.

But everyone was ready to do what needed to be done.

Nobody asked for anything special.

Nobody is to blame for getting surprised that we ended up in Baqubah.

None of that matters when you get home and the hardest part of making it through the day is waiting to hear the next explosion or burst of machine gun fire on the street. Marshall's book is another chapter that tells us how it feels for a regular person to endure this kind of experience and try to put yourself back together.

Lieutenant Colonel David Pearson
October 2019

Introduction

I am on a plane, dinner has been served and eaten, they've just turned out the lights and everyone around me is getting a few winks or watching *The Rock* or reruns of *The Office* – but I am sitting here pondering how to introduce the book you now hold in your hands.

It's a pretty good question - I am a film director; I am not a military person and I have never been to war, so the contents of this book are a long way outside of any experience that I have ever had... So, what I'm wondering is what I can add, what perspective of mine would be appropriate; in short, how I should go about introducing you to the world of Aaron Marshall.

I have known Aaron for the last two years, due to his involvement in a film I was making, a comedy horror called *Deep Clean*, but I believe the real reason he made contact was because of the impact on him of a previous film of mine, *American The Bill Hicks Story*, a documentary biopic of the infamous outlaw comic.

I say the impact of the film, but of course what I really mean is that he had connected with Bill's work - his sense of humor and world view, scathing yet loving, profound yet profane, and that wonderful knack he had for distilling complex issues down to a joke, which succeeds not only in making you laugh, but turning your understanding of that issue on its head.

Bill of course had some famously strong (and at the time, rather controversial) opinions on the first Gulf War, and perhaps what may have resonated for Aaron – who was caught up in the middle of the second one – was having a voice in his ear letting him know that perhaps he wasn't the only one who thought there might just be a disparity between what the government, the mainstream media, and the military leadership were saying and what was really going on...

I assume that it did because he has included his own self-drawn comic strips of a scene between himself and Bill discussing the reasons for the war. I sincerely hope that Bill's words were of some comfort to him as the shells were flying over his head.

And so, it seems we have arrived at the book you now hold in your hands…

This is not a normal book, and that is as it should be.

The experiences recounted within are indeed far from normal. It's a story about conflict and what happens to young men and women involved in fighting far from home, for motivations that became murkier as time went on, and after an extended period of boredom, interspersed with occasional extreme violence, what happens when they get back home - just trying to get on with their lives, coping with the basic, and the everyday, whilst trying to remember what "normal" felt like.

Baqubah: Bones and Blood is one young man's attempt to deal with, and understand that experience – by examining it, writing about it, recording it, filtering it through other artists, comedians, and musicians that mattered to him, to understand, to process, and perhaps, one day, at some point, to move on.

How would you go about doing this? I mean you, personally? Would you tell it like it was? The righteous ire reserved for presidents who lie and fight wars to impress their fathers is easy enough. The hard part comes when faced with analyzing one's own behavior.

Would the temptation be there to paint yourself a little more heroic, to omit some of the things that weren't perhaps part of your ideal narrative, to include the horrors you have seen but perhaps omit the off-color jokes you made afterward to cope with it? To describe the charred bodies, but leave out the drinking and not always exemplary behavior of one's own?

A completely natural human instinct - but that is not the path Aaron takes…

Instead he realizes, as Bill realized, that admitting to the darker, more disturbing aspects of one's own psyche is the only way that others might

14

be helped through the same process by the simple realization that one is not alone in the dark – others have felt this too, and that is honorable and to be applauded.

Aaron's recollections of his time in the conflict were born of diaries, audio recordings, and his own experiences which truly mine that place that we might call the juxtaposition of the mad and the mundane, and for me this is the value of the work he has produced.

Aaron peppers his recollections with standout moments that jar and pull you up – just when you thought you were getting a Platoon-style horror of war story, he breaks it up with excursions into amusing pornography mix-ups, growing relations with the locals, soldier-on-soldier violence, and his own misdeeds that suddenly throw you out of the story you thought you were in, and into a whole new set of issues.

This is then contrasted with the effects of what is happening to him, in unflinching and honest detail, back home – on breaks between tours and afterwards as he attempts to deal with PTSD by drinking, fighting, flashing his gun at random annoying traffic users at stop lights, and generally losing the plot.

Stylistically, there are echoes in the use of disjointed time slices of works such as Vonnegut's *Slaughterhouse Five*, or perhaps those parts of *Apocalypse Now* which attempt to derail your senses and put you in the first person driving seat of an experience that seems at once a million miles away, and yet oddly familiar (from all those war movies of course, not the real thing) but ultimately, *Baqubah: Bones and Blood* is very much its own beast.

Aaron's retelling of these events have that odor – of valor in possibly senseless circumstances, of loyalty and compassion for his comrades and those around him, and finally of a genuine and heartfelt human need to try and make sense of it all by engaging in this – a creative process, an outpouring of facts and dreams and recollections and emotions, in an attempt to reclaim not only his humanity but to cling on to his sanity.

It is an unfiltered, firsthand report from the frontlines of human experience. It is raw, and odd, and disturbing, and funny, and strange, and very real.

As Hunter S. Thompson, the head gonzo reporter himself once said, "When the going gets weird, the weird turn pro."

He might've been talking about this book.

Matt Harlock
Somewhere 36,000ft above the Earth
Nov 2019

CONTENTS

A Message for You

I hope standing next to my psyche as I retell numerous traumatic events from the front lines of the Iraq War opens your mind up in some fashion.

My goal is to convince anyone who needs convincing that life is worth living and everything will be okay. We all go through some sort of trauma. And maybe you think what happened to me is far worse than your traumatic experiences.

But I think that's the trick to recovering from trauma; The realization that others have been through far worse and have still led productive, meaningful and happy lives.

Others have also been through less and died.

I truly didn't feel like I had any right to publish a book because of that worthless feeling anyone who has ever experienced trauma knows well.

If you have ever been in that place, or perhaps are now, know that I have felt that too. You are not alone. And this book is my proof.

Chapter 1 Memories and Dreams

"It is by no means an irrational fancy that, in a future existence, we shall look upon what we think our present existence, as a dream." –Edgar Allen Poe

That baby's crying non-stop and I'm pretty sure if they don't shut the goddamn thing up, we're fucked. I have no idea how to get out of this house. The layout was supposed to be the same as that shithole we just searched two blocks over.

"If she doesn't shut that fucking baby up, I'm going to shut it up for her. I can promise you that."

"Jesus Christ, Aaron!" said Houston.

"Sorry, sorry. I've just had a long goddamn shift and I'd like to make it back to the station to smoke at least one fucking cigarette today where there isn't a chance of one of us getting shot in the face at the same fucking time ".

The sand got into everything in the desert. It wasn't so bad in the city, but that didn't stop me from daydreaming about moments in my life where I did enjoy sand. One night as a fourteen-year-old boy in Cocoa Beach, Florida, I hung out with a local girl I met earlier in the day. She had golden blonde hair that made you forget your thoughts as they silhouetted her green eyes and that childish smile only a fourteen-year-old boy can truly appreciate. It was past sunset, and she showed me how if you rub your fingers through the sand at night you can watch it glow. We did this numerous times and the image of her running her hands with mine through the sand is something I'll never forget. The wind forced our eyes to meet, although another primal reason other than personal safety can be attributed to that.

The salt air smelled as sweet as the young woman I was with.

I thought of this often in Iraq. The cold screams of the invisible birds off in the distance. The sound of water rising and falling; never failing, like it knows its purpose and will continue to rumble long after I'm gone. The soft glow of tiny rocks beneath fingertips touching for the first time. So, when anyone brought up how much they hated sand – and the usual jokes about it getting into every crevasse of your body and belongings would come up – I would just silently think to myself: I like sand, especially the sand I was introduced to that night 7 years before as a teenager in Cocoa Beach. And it would make me smile.

We arrived in the desert oasis of Baqubah on March 25th, 2004. And our first real taste of combat would come the very next day via an RPG (**Anti-Tank Rocket**) attack. 'What a great way to start the tour,' I thought. 'This should be one hell of a year.'

Luckily, I have the memory, notes, and recordings of myself and the soldiers I served with that sheds a lot of light on what it was really like to be in Baqubah, Iraq in early 2004 to February 2005. We got to participate in so many fun activities. It was just like the movie *Step Brothers*. Hey, I never asked you, do you like guacamole?

Finally, A moment to collect my thoughts.

The barracks, if you want to call them that, were just out of the wretched condition we found them in. Over an inch of dirt and debris were piled up around the rooms like the previous owners had ransacked the place in a drunken rage. The windows hadn't been bricked up yet and you could still see to the east of the city through the screened windows. Finally... a chance to collect my thoughts and try to make sense of what the hell I was doing in this shithole, when another large explosion rocked the building.

Every goddamn item I had placed on the dresser against the east wall went flying off. Probably another RPG. Sweet. I guess this isn't going to be a moment where I breathe easy. And that's how most days went. Just when you thought you could catch your breath; another fucking situation came up.

We all dealt with trauma on a regular basis in Baqubah. Trauma is one way of saying it.

Some fucked up shit happened.

Some.

Fucked.

Up.

Shit.

And we all handled dealing with that fucked up shit very differently while we were in Iraq and when we returned to the States. Could more have been done to prepare us for the onslaught that PTSD had to offer? Could more be done to prevent it from happening to soldiers who are returning from combat now? Could the Army have prepared us better?

The answer to all these questions is of course, yes.

Should Secular Chaplains be allowed to help those soldiers who don't happen to believe in magical thinking, and might the cause of many preventable suicides be the fact the soldiers simply have no one to talk to that isn't non-secular in some way? Too many of my Brothers and Sisters at Arms have taken their own lives. Why is this? Why are so many continuing to do this daily? Is there anything we can do about it?

The answer to the last question is yes. We can do something about it. The other two questions aren't as easy to answer, but hopefully by the end of this, we'll have some.

I'll show the reasons I used to convince myself that suicide was a valid option. Which, in turn, will hopefully make those of us that still feel alone, and happen to read this, see that there is hope for a better life.

We should also take steps to ensure that we're doing everything humanly possible to prevent veteran suicide. Whether it's sharing a Facebook post about PTSD awareness, which is a great start, to the real help, which is by spreading the right knowledge to the right people. By always letting your brothers and sisters at arms know that you are there for them, and they are not alone.

Operation Reboot Outdoors is a prime example. We are not alone. There is always a reason to live. Even if you don't believe the words. Repeat them to yourself like a motherfucking mantra. Be hypnotized by life. Because as far as any of us know for certain, we are only given one. I mean it would be sweet to be reincarnated as a bonobo, the gentle great ape that happens to be our closest living relative in the animal kingdom. Those beautiful bastards use sex as a way of greeting each other. Imagine that! Not everything cool has been kept by evolution and lets just leave it at that...

Chapter 2 Baqubah Iraq

"I don't think of all the misery, but of the beauty that still remains." -Anne Frank

Producer says over the intercom, "What are you doing? Why is it taking so long?"

Aaron, "Squirrels man, in the belfry, it's the worst case I've ever seen! Give me a fucking minute!"

Producer, "I'm coming in."

The Producer bursts into the recording space and sees me trying to cook up a dose of heroin in a spoon. I was crying out for help back then and I didn't even realize it. At first, he looked genuinely disappointed, but that faded quickly, and his face turned to rage... Somehow, though, he kept it together.

"Dude. Get out. Get out now. Take all that shit and get out. Whatever the fuck you're doing with your little science experiment from hell, grab it all up, okay, and leave my studio this fucking second."

"What the fuck man? Am I supposed to just go out to the common area outside the studio and shoot up like a junky in the goddamn hallway!?

The Producer, "You are a junky"

"You know what Frank? You can take that Ak-47 I gave you and shove it right up your ass."

I never apologized to him for being such a piece of shit, but I'm apologizing now. You were always just trying to do what was best for me. You came and saw me in Portland when nobody *else would. You got me out of bed most mornings when I didn't want to make a record by yelling at me over the phone and swearing at me until I was motivated. You got me into the studio, and you helped make it happen. I wouldn't have just made #13 on Bull Moose's list of Best-Selling Local Artists of the Decade without you.*

As I'm writing about this old friend who I had a falling out with for different reasons, I shit you not, one of his sons messages me. He reminds me of going out to Applebee's with his Dad and I when he was kid. We would often talk about music, work, and life in general. He says he remembers nothing but good things, and man did that make me smile. Then he goes on to tell me I should make some more music. He has always enjoyed my work and would love to see me make a record again.

I mean immediately I'm staring something right in the face. That's two generations of actual saints cheering me on to make music. For an Atheist like myself, that's a hard-goddamn pill to swallow.

Baqubah, Iraq.

What kind of fucked up name is that?

Well I guess it's better than being in Dildo, Canada, or Wank, Germany. Pussy, France might be nice though. But no, Baqubah, Iraq is where we ended up from March of 2004 until February of 2005.

I tattooed the city's name on me when I returned stateside, strangely enough because it became my home for a year, our home, and I never wanted to forget that home. Regardless of the horrors I would be a part of. We would fight damn hard during that time to make sure it stayed our home, regardless of the trauma.

Regardless.

But we can get into more of how that came to be later.

Do you think there's a Pussy House of Pizza in that town in France? I hope so. My childish humor would love it and the American in me says, 'Hell Yeah! Pussy and Pizza!'

Okay. Where was I?

On April 7th, 2004 we were standing around at F.O.B. Warhorse on QRF (**Quick Reaction Force**) duty when we got a call over the radio there was a "Black Hawk Down" near the Police Station. It turned out to be a Kiowa Warrior. Of course, in our minds all we could think of was the movie *Black Hawk Down*, and that didn't end well for a lot of them. A lot of them.

From what I could remember about the movie, the turret gunners had one hell of a job during that mission, and that was rushing through my mind as I was standing in my turret headed towards the downed helicopter. We were in a city, and the number of hostiles in the area was unknown. But if they had just taken one of our birds down, it was likely there were more than a couple of them still lurking about. In a city of a couple hundred thousand people, who knew how the situation might turn out? And I can guarantee you none of us had any idea how it would end.

We hadn't been in Baqubah that long, so this was our first sip of dealing directly with the Iraqi people during a hostile situation. Luckily neither one of the two U.S. Pilots were killed or seriously injured. They had ripped some Iraqis out of a car and were attempting to drive to a base when some of the first responders found them and gave them some much needed help. The crowds of people were what I remember. Right before the wave of gunfire that sounded like a thousand ball bearings being thrown hard into the mind of a schizophrenic, but I'll get to that in a minute.

The crowds were starting to form, and we were trying to keep everyone away from the area. We knew there were insurgents around because the "helo" was shot down by enemy fire, so they were still probably in the immediate area, possibly getting ready to do a secondary attack on us or to try and get at the aircraft. This was the first time we had to deal with any of this shit. And nothing had prepared us for it. This type of situation was not covered in our training at Ft. Dix.

I still couldn't speak any Arabic and we didn't have any interpreters with us. As the crowds started to get closer to the area, I had to keep clear, I pointed my rifle directly at the growing mob and yelled as loud as I could, "Get the fuck

31

back!" If they didn't understand English, it didn't matter. My weapon pointed directly at their beaks sent the message loud and clear...

It took me a minute to even get the courage to do this because as I was looking at all of them, I was thinking that these were all civilians just trying to get a closer look at the situation. I mean a helicopter had fucking crashed in their neighborhood. If a helicopter kissed dirt in a downtown Boston filled with foreigners, I'm sure Larry Warren and his crew would be one of the first to come out and see what the fuck was going on.

But then it hit me that someone in the area had just shot this son of a bitch down.

Jesus Christ.

Maybe it was one of the people I was now trying to keep away from the wreckage. Maybe it was that Iraqi kid that looked strangely like my childhood neighbor Spencer Berry in such a weird way I had to look back at him over a half-dozen times.

Sgt. Ryan Trahan was on top of OP 1 (Footnote Observation Post) at the Police Station when all of this was going on and he saw the Kiowa get shot down. Thinking back on the event he says it was like watching it on instant reply. It circled over the blue dome nearby, which was another U.S. occupied Iraqi government building, and was heading back to where it came from when some enemy fire hit the rotor of the helicopter. He saw the goddamn thing get hit and thought the helicopter might come crashing down on him for a moment. Imagine seeing that shit? It's just wild. You must be goddamn close to feel like that. And he was.

It ended up landing about 400-meters away from him, luckily in a nearby field. He recalls the chaos of people yelling and shouting in the streets and that's about the same time I showed up to secure the area with the QRF team. Then some Bradley's or "tracks" as we called them, came rolling in from FOB (**Forward Operating Base**) Gabe.

As I was trying to control the crowd, the Bradley's lit up their 20mm guns along with every other soldier in the area. It sounded like pure madness. I was facing the opposite direction of the gunfire and remember turning around towards it and thinking, 'What the fuck!?' I'm trying to keep a crowd of Iraqis at bay while I'm worrying that an attack might happen and then more gunfire erupts than I had ever heard in my entire life.

It wasn't even comparable to anything I had ever heard before. It wasn't even close. My brain couldn't comprehend what the fuck was going on. All I could do was watch the U.S. Soldiers light up a target down the road and watch the Iraqis I had been trying to hold back run for their lives. They sure as shit weren't interested in what was going on here anymore. And if I didn't have a job to do, I would have been joining them.

Shit, where's the Chai? Let's go have some tea and talk about the weather.

The gunfire was being directed at a vehicle that tried to run a roadblock and was quickly turned into a moving metal magnet for every American machine gun. Unfortunately, it also had two people inside. Humans.

The gentlemen driving was the son of a high-ranking Iraqi Officer and he thought he didn't have to listen to our warnings to stay back from the area. He was wrong. And it was a very unfortunate death... Another case of someone making an unfortunately poor decision in a time of War. Much like the time an Iraqi was shot off his bicycle after turning the corner to where an intense firefight was taking place. I may say more about that later. But things like this happen in War. And it's important we understand that so that we can try to make sure things like that never happen again. Some things though, are just unavoidable. War makes sure of that.

One of the passengers in the vehicle lay dead and naked sprawled out half-hazard in the gutter when I pulled up in my Humvee near the roadblock. The other guy was still alive. I could count at least 20 bullet holes in him, but he was still breathing. Asking for water.

'I'm sorry,' I thought, *but that isn't going to help you. And the water I gave him seemed to drain through his body like a strainer.*

I think it was because I became more focused on his blood loss when he started to drink, which gave the illusion of water going in his mouth, down his weakening throat and out his body in over two dozen different directions instead of the usual one. It was disturbing to see someone cling to life after such a brutal shooting.

We were taking him to F.O.B. Warhorse when we saw an Iraqi ambulance on our way. So, we flagged them down to get him quicker medical care. But when the ambulance opened the back doors it was immediately clear this man's chances of survival were gone. There wasn't anything inside the ambulance. No medical equipment. No EMT's in professional uniforms ready to save a life. It was more like a hearse.

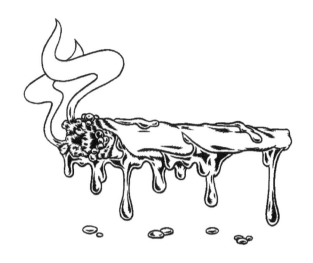

Chapter 3 Roger That

Ft. Dix, New Jersey

"Two things are infinite; the universe and human stupidity; and I'm not sure about the universe." –
Albert Einstein

The following is an actual email sent to me by Jim Watson in 2016.

"I remember thinking 'how the fuck am I going to treat this?'

Her arm was hanging by strands and bone, and blood was everywhere. I just started reacting and doing what I felt might help.

I wrapped her arm in gauze and she was given morphine. She kept yelling at me not to put a tourniquet on her. I told her that I was not putting a tourniquet on her, but did not have the heart to tell her that her arm was almost gone...

I remember everyone watching and encouraging both. We got them into an ambulance, and I thought my job was done. I was wrong. They told me that I was going to evacuate them to warhorse as the team lead.

"Are you fucking kidding me!" I said.

The ride seemed very long, and I remember being scared out of my mind that we would be hit again. The window was partway down, and I was having a panic attack because it would not go up. I never did get it up. We arrived safely and unloaded them to awaiting doctors and medics. I then broke down, crying and hysterical. The medical 1st Sergeant came over and hugged me and told me I did great and probably saved her life. I didn't' feel that way. I thought I could've done more and been way more prepared.

We were originally a Field Artillery unit from the New Hampshire Army National Guard. Then the Army, in its infinite wisdom, decided to train us as Military Police officers in the snow, in the middle of winter, in New Jersey, to fight a war in the desert...

I'm not saying some logical steps weren't properly taken here, but somebody did some piss poor planning.

We were being trained mostly by men and women who had never seen any combat or even been to the desert. There were several who served in the initial taking of Iraq, but they were few and far between. For the most part, we were being trained by intellectually deficient self-absorbed assholes who cared more about being right than teaching us a goddamn thing.

There was one class we took for combat medic training, where the instructor said, "hooah," no less than 53 times in a half hour. I counted. After about the 20th time he said it, I started saying it back and he would say "hooah" even louder and became even more enthusiastic about it.

I'm not saying this guy was a bad instructor. But the only thing I remembered about the class after taking it was that if one of your brothers in arms gets a fucking chest wound then, "hooah!"...

It was so cold at Ft. Dix in the winter of 2003. So frikken cold.

We were constantly waiting for buses that were forever late. It was an amazing time to be in the Army. *I drank whiskey throughout most of the days to stay warm. I don't recommend it.* Some comments about the cold from fellow soldiers about the situation at Ft. Dix are as follows;

- There will be warming tents, maybe. Eat chow and stand outside with your gear for an extra hour and wait for the bus to decide to show up. (Steve Robbins)
- Well at least it will be realistic and useful training that will help us complete our mission. (Jon Foote)
- I seem to remember stuffing newspapers in my uniform like a homeless person would do for added insulation. And a cardboard box would have been warmer than an Army warming tent. (Chris St. Marie)
- You don't remember all the IED's that the insurgents hid in the snow? (John Boissonneau)
- The day on the MK19 range was awesome in a foot of snow. (David Huckins)
- It wasn't snow; it was camouflaged sand. (Chris St. Marie)

The word "Roger" is a very common term used in the military. But some of us in Baqubah decided to give the word a new meaning. We used to think of it as meaning. "Go fuck yourself" or "fuck you" or "suck my cock asshole" ... Any of these derogatory meanings would work. It gave us a morale boost after we were told to do something that was completely idiotic. But it's the Army, and that's the nature of it. So, we would just reply, "Roger," and do what we were told, smiling all the way.

We trained in the goddamn snow. In the snow.

That was supposedly going to get us ready to fight a war in a desert, in extreme heat.

During one of our training missions we were learning how to cordon off areas and we had all started to get a little bored. We were all cold and tired. But that didn't stop me from having a little fun. I was standing about 80 feet away from Sgt. Smiliak in the turret of another vehicle, when he decided to finally grab something to eat and pulled out a package of potato sticks that he had been looking forward to all day. Afterall, it's the Army, the small things can matter a lot sometimes...

I casually made a snowball and decided to see if I could hit the Humvee that he was in. Well, my aim happened to be a little too good that day. When I launched the ice ball it went down through the turret of Smilaik's vehicle and directly into the package of potato sticks that he was holding in his hand.

Suddenly we heard, "fuck! Who the fuck did that!" and he came running over pissed as hell to find out who did it?

He blamed Rhodes for throwing it because he was the first person he saw when he walked over. I just kept my mouth shut. And we all had a good laugh over it.

Machine gun Ricky would get the last laugh though. I asked the marine if I could stash my growing collection of roaches in his room, which was in a separate building than ours, but still within our compound. For a few reasons. But there was one thing I didn't think of. After a month of handing off delicious bits of bud to him, I finally asked for them back. He laughed. I will never forget the look on his goddamn face. He then said he smoked them all and just kind of stood there casually saying sorry, the only way I think a marine knows how. With his body language. Then a few low apathetic grunts. I thought of the ice ball incident at fort Dix and my rage turned into a smile, thanks to my close lifelong friend, Karma.

Chapter 4 April 9th, 2004

"Even God cannot change the past." –Agathon

April 9th, 2004 was like a fucking blizzard in a pot of coffee. And not that k-cup shit. I'm talking old school Dunkin' Donuts commercial from the 80's kind of coffee.

Thick, chewy and dripping like burnt tobacco.

The memories come back to me in pieces. The most vivid as snapshots in time, so clear I feel like I could reach out and touch them.

Yet just as I reach, the image turns into vapor and slips between my fingertips.

I was hit three different times by near direct RPG blasts and was wounded by some shrapnel.

Fun fact: The words "shrapnel" actually comes from Major General Henry Shrapnel who was a British Officer who invented the "Shrapnel Shell" a couple hundred years ago.

But back to my shrapnel wound...

I didn't get medical attention for it, and I stayed on duty until long after the fight was over. The moments I remember most clearly happened directly before the battle even started, and I say "battle," because that is exactly what it fucking was.

A Special Forces soldier that fought beside me that day would end up receiving the Silver Star.

The building we were stationed at in Baqubah was the Provincial Police Station. It was a small two-story brick building that had a large amount of failing white and light blue paint that screamed to come off. It was surrounded by hesco barriers topped with barbed wire with only one main gate but nestled in the back and side were two smaller entrances to the compound.

The roof of the building had five main vantagepoints. Four on the corners and one on the south side that was a crow's-nest (an elevated tower), which gave the best vantagepoint of all but left whoever was in it completely exposed to the enemy during an attack.

We had little more than a few sandbags for cover at each observation post. In fact, the day after this firefight, Specialist Jameson Holmes and myself filled and carried over 150 sandbags to the roof to fortify the positions. Later, some Iraqi contractors would build a three-foot wall around the entire roof. This relieved a lot of the anxiety I had about the piss poor cover.

But on April 9th, 2004 the wall didn't yet exist, and I happened to be stationed on top of OP 4 facing the southwest behind a few dozen filthy dirt-filled sandbags.

Of course, it didn't matter what goddamn direction you were facing. You could have been kneeling with your head towards Mecca and you were still about to have the single worst day of your life. The last. In fact, that's exactly how it turned out.

Earlier in the day we were briefed that an attack was coming, so when my shift came, I started to think about what that might look like and where the assault might come from. If I was the enemy, where would I attack from and still have a great escape route? Because most times we were attacked, the enemy ran away just as quickly as they appeared – like they were trained by David Blaine and knew the secrets of invisibility...

Another soldier and I were talking this over when we noticed one dirt road that was perfect to retreat from. The road started about 100-meters from the compound and led straight away from the city, and the police station. We just stared at the corner of that road and the wall that led beside it. It was unusually hot, and we hadn't been in the country for too long, but I thought I was starting to get accustomed to the weather. The dirt seemed to whorl off the ground, with the heat making it almost impossible to breathe. 15 minutes had passed and then I saw it... To this day that image is still burnt into my mind like a stamp forever pressed into my memory.

For a moment I saw the tip of an RPG poke out behind the wall then dip back behind it. I had never trained for a situation where I saw the enemy accidentally show where they were by dipping the end of an RPG just past a wall, but my instincts took over. And by instincts, I mean training.

Confused yet? You should be. But stay with me.

The training I'm talking about is the training I received in Basic Training at Ft. Sill in Oklahoma just a few months prior.

You see the enemy, you kill them. Lesson over.

After seeing the enemy, I put down the binoculars and reached for my weapon while I screamed at the top of my lungs, "RPG!!"

I have no idea why I decided to scream that out, but it came out as loud and fast as I could muster.

As I looked down the top of my barrel to where I was going to shoot, there was a man on his knees, pointing an RPG directly at me. I let loose a small burst of rounds, and then I can remember thinking how cartoonish an RPG looks coming at you.

The memory comes back to me just how it happened. Like an infinite amount of time could pass while the repeating picture of a rocket comes straight at you and flashes over and over.

Time seems to stop when I think about it, and time seemed to stop at the exact moment it happened. Regardless of what people say, you can see the goddamn thing for a split second. Maybe I could see it because I use to be an artillery man and you can see the rounds coming out of a howitzer if you are standing in the right spot. It's incredible.

The fear wasn't there. The fear comes after.

The fear always came after a firefight or battle took place. When you sit alone and think back to what happened you say to yourself, 'holy shit, how the fuck am I still alive?' And those thoughts cause the fear.

The fear never took hold during a firefight. Fuck. *I always had too much shit to do during combat to worry about whether I should be afraid.* And I always got really pissed off that people were trying to kill me. It fucking got under my skin.

After the explosion, I got up half thinking I was dead and dreaming and saw the man who shot the cartoon rocket at me sprawled out on the ground, flat on his back with his knees bent. Another man ran across from the body and ducked behind a dump truck. I sat down behind the sandbags to reload and the other soldier who was with me on the OP got hit with an RPG explosion directly below his position. I literally saw him get blown back by the concussion of that rocket.

I asked him, or yelled at him – because you couldn't hear shit due to all the goddamn gunfire and explosions – "are you alright?"

He nodded 'yes,' and we both kept fighting.

I can still see the look of blue holy shit in his eyes surrounded by an ocean of white what the fuck.

Some people think that being in combat must feel like an eternity. The reality of it is, when heavy fighting is taking place, it seems as if it only lasts for a few minutes when hours have passed.

This could also have a lot to do with the fact I was hit so hard by so many explosions I blacked out for periods of time and only really remember this entire day in pictures from my mind. A little flip book of horror.

It always comes back choppy and in pieces. Specific moments get rearranged in my mind over time. I don't know how many RPG's were fired at us that day (some reports say 25, some say 45), but it was worthy of a grand finale during the fourth of July.

It was a gloriously evil and dark event that was beautiful at the same time. It's like falling in love with a painting only to be told it was done by Adolf Hitler. But we held our ground. We got beat down hard that day, but they didn't get inside that compound; our compound. Our home.

The crow's-nest, which was a 15 ft. tower on the southernmost side of the building, was hit directly by an RPG and one of the Special Forces guys who fought with us that day ended up crawling out of it pretty much intact with his spirits high. You could see the glow of excitement emanating from his face. It was like his aura was projecting itself out at you. Those guys were jacked up after that fight.

One of them said, "Man, we have seen some shit in Iraq, but nothing compares to this!"

At that moment I realized I had a long goddamn tour ahead of me, because we had only been in Baqubah for a few weeks, and if a Special Forces guy was saying this was the craziest shit he had ever seen, I couldn't imagine it getting any better.

And it didn't.

During the night of April 9th, some soldiers were sitting around near the jail telling stories about the battle that day and just trying to comprehend what the hell had happened.

Foote and Trahan were there, indulging in conversation when a rat came out from under the walls and went straight towards what appeared to be a piece of one of the inmate's intestines who was shot point blank earlier in the day during the riot that happened simultaneously as the insurgent's direct assault. Everyone just stared at the rat and watched it drag its prize away.

Just another great moment in Baqubah.

What's that over there? Oh nothing, just some human flesh.

Chapter 5 Absinthian Dreams

"Truth is never pure, and rarely simple." –Oscar Wilde

Some things just don't need to be said. And this is probably one of those things.

I paid an Iraqi police officer who was also a friend of mine $50 for some porno tapes. But something must have gotten completely fucking lost in translation, because when he showed up the next day, they were homemade porno tapes of him and his wife. That made for one of the most socially awkward moments of my entire tour.

He didn't seem to care at all that I was about to see him disgustingly mount his wife as she giggled, laughed, and moaned. In fact, I don't think I had ever seen him look any happier than when he handed me the tapes, smiling from ear to ear. I just assumed that he had found some good pornography. But as I would soon find out, one person's idea of good porn can be wildly different from another's.

Needless to say, I stopped buying pornography from my Iraqi friends after that.

Before we arrived in Iraq, we still didn't know our orders. Well, let me put it this way, the men who were ranked as low as myself still didn't know our orders. All we knew was that we were recently retrained as Military Police Officers and told we were going to war. Well fuck me ragged. It wasn't easy getting on that plane. And it was even harder to get back on another one after I took my two weeks leave in July of 2004 and knew exactly what I was heading back into.

During my two week leave from the War, as I was driving around New Hampshire with my first ex-wife, eating steak three times a day and trying to enjoy the immense amount of security and safety we take for granted in our everyday lives in America, I kept thinking this: What if I just swerved off the road and hit a tree? Maybe I would get injured enough so I wouldn't have to go back to Iraq? I might die as well, but there might be a better chance I'll survive and get to stay in America.

I probably would have done that too, if it wasn't for one thing. What about all the soldiers that I would leave behind? Would it be fair to leave them in Iraq to do even more work on my behalf because I was selfish and wanted to stay in the States?

The answer is no.

When we lost guys in Iraq due to injuries and other reasons of that nature, we didn't always get replacements. Christ, come to think of it, I think we only got one replacement during the entire tour. And the more guys that left, the more work we then had to do in return. I had signed up for the War in Iraq, and I would see it through to the end.

We were 33,000 feet over Iraq, and I can still remember seeing all these fires on the ground. I knew we were over Iraq because the pilot announced it. When you fly over the U.S. at night you see lights in uniform shapes and can make out what you are looking at by the amount of lights on the ground. Oh, there's a city. Or, oh there's a small town. How cute. But over this landscape, all I was seeing was random fires, some big and some small. But just fires. Flickering billowing flames that danced and mingled in the dark of night. It looked completely alien to me.

These were the moments where I asked myself what the hell, I had really gotten myself into. As gung-ho as I was to do something for my country after the attacks on the World Trade Centers on September 11th, I still had moments of complete uncertainty in what I was *doing*.

Was I trained well enough? How would I handle actual combat? Would I even see any combat? Would I be lucky enough to not see any?

All these questions and more would be answered in the coming year.

And one phrase that helped me in times of trouble was something my mother used to say to me when times were tough, "This too shall pass."

'This too shall pass... This too shall pass...' I said that to myself a thousand times and more throughout the War. And sure enough, after 452 days, it did.

During the flight into Kuwait I took my boots off to try and get a little more comfortable. When I went to put them back on something strange had happened. I thought I grabbed someone else's boots because I couldn't slide my feet in. Shit. Did I somehow accidentally switch boots with someone by mistake during the flight? Nope. My feet had swollen up so much during the flight that I couldn't fit them in properly.

Somehow, I did end up getting the fuckers on just before we landed in Kuwait. Ahhhh Kuwait, land of the... shit... I don't know.

The only thing I had ever learned about Kuwait was that we gave them a hand when Saddam tried to take over their oil fields during the Gulf War in the early 90's. Yeah, hot and sunny Kuwait. Except we landed at night, so it was just insanely hot. But I would beg for the coolness of 90-degree weather after I experienced the extent to which the sun can beat a man down in the sands of Iraq during the summer.

Outside the TOC (Tactical Operations Command) in Baqubah, they posted a weekly weather report which always made me laugh, and I occasionally had to say, 'wait a minute' to someone, while I went and checked the weather.

Oh, another seven straight days of sunshine and no clouds. Sweet! Another personal weather anomaly that still blows my mind to this day, is the day that I realized I had forgotten what rain felt like.

It was just another bright sunny day in Baqubah, when suddenly, I was being attacked by tiny mosquitos of some sort. These fuckers were vicious and wanted blood! What the hell!? What swarm of fuckery is this!?

I swatted at my arms for a few seconds like an insane person until I realized it was rain. I had forgotten what rain felt like. Jesus Christ.

Let that sink in for a minute. I sure did.

At that moment I couldn't have felt any farther from my loved ones. But when moments like that happened, I would just turn to my wedding ring and rub the gold raw.

Thump. Thump. Thump. Thump. Thump. Thump... The sound of my daughter's heartbeat, recorded while still in her mother's belly, calmed me down more than a Norah Jones record. And that was some feat seeing that the only way I could ever sleep was by playing one of her records and putting on headphones.

We worked seven days a week for a year straight in Baqubah. My eye also started to twitch about halfway through the tour. It never did that before. When I get stressed now my eye will still twitch, or if I even think about what happened in Iraq it will twitch.

It's twitching right now.

Thump. Thump. Thump. That was my child's heartbeat on the recording, and once I heard that tape, I knew I had to make it back home. One out of every six of the U.S. Soldiers serving at the Baqubah Provincial Police Station would receive the Purple Heart by the end of the tour. Thump. Thump. It's all I could think about for the next few weeks in between the constant threat of IED's, firefights, ambushes, RPG's, and mortar attacks.

It's a hell of thing to be shaken out of a daydream by the thud of a mortar round, or the blast of an RPG. It's also a hell of a thing to be in such a dangerous place with your mind back home. So, I pushed thoughts of home away the best I could, the best any of us could, because we all had a job to do.

One of my favorite "jobs" was what we liked to call, "taking out the trash." This was code for when a few friends and I would hypothetically go outside behind the dumpsters which were burning twenty-four hours a day (burn pits... awesome), to smoke a joint.

Sometimes we wouldn't have any trash to bring out so we would ask other soldiers in the building if they wanted us to bring their trash down. They always said yes, and they never asked why. I don't think I'd ask why or say no if someone wanted to bring my trash down either, we already had enough shit to deal with. Someone taking out the trash was a welcomed five-minute break for any one of us. It was one of the few moments in Iraq where you could forget where you are, forget where you'll be tomorrow, and just breath in the present.

Mmmmmm. Burn pit smoke and marijuana. So lovely.

How did we get good homegrown marijuana on the front lines of Iraq you might ask? Well, hypothetically speaking you had a few options.

One way for example, was for a soldier who went on leave to the States to have the testicular fortitude to package up a bunch of pot and mail it to himself in the warzone.

What? Yeah. That could happen.

You just buy a bunch of packages of pens and highlighters (highlighters work better because they are a bit larger than pens and can hold larger joints). The downside to highlighters is that you can't take the felt tip out of it since it would look fishy if someone took the cap off, so some of the pink, green and yellow ink that is still inside leaks into the joints and you end up with brightly colored blunts.

Smoking a pink, green or yellow doobie in the sands of Iraq is a surreal experience, or so I'm told.

Some soldiers got a lot of packages of pens during the tour, well, one soldier. But he just liked writing, and he ran out of ink a lot. A lot.

Another option is taking out all the tobacco in one pack of cigarettes and replacing it with pot. Then putting the pack back in a carton and shipping it over, so if the carton gets checked, the chances of that one pack being spotted are slim.

But who would do something like that? Certainly not me.

Some people say you never get used to the smell of Iraq. But those of us in Baqubah got used to it. It could have to do with the fact we had a burn pit going 24-hours a day for the entire tour which left our sense of smell squashed. After a few months of the constant odor, you might as well have hit us all directly in the nose with a sledgehammer. We also spent every day outside in the city, and like living near a paper mill town where I grew up (Rumford, Mexico, Peru, and Dixfield), you eventually get used to the smell after a while, only noticing it when it gets extremely bad.

Silence and then shock. An extremely loud explosion followed by the sight of dust instantly releasing itself from the ceiling and walls. The exact moment it happens it's hard to comprehend what you are witnessing. I had never seen all the dust from a structure instantaneously remove itself from the surface it once rested on in such a violent fashion.

It's just another RPG slamming into the side of the Baqubah Provincial police station, or a mortar round dropping brutally from above. It happened daily when we first arrived. But only if you happened to be staring at the ceiling at the exact right moment would you witness this peculiarly beautiful event.

Within the first few weeks of arriving in Baqubah I would end up killing people for the first time in my life. Humans.

I didn't seek these people out to shoot at. They were trying to kill me. Trying to kill us.

Everyone I ended up killing during my tour had shot at me first, and this is how I am able to deal with it. Others I served with were not so lucky.

The flight from New Jersey to Atlanta was your typical hurry up and wait scenario that is known all too well by anyone who has ever worn a uniform. I was sitting in one of the forever-waiting lines that form in the Army, when I thought, 'well fuck me gently with a chainsaw, there's 50 Cent.' And sure, as shit it was him. The rapper walked by as we waited in one of the concourses. He was smiling from ear to ear.

The only thing I know for sure about 50 Cent is that the dude is like an international bank, and if he wants his money you better pay him by Monday.

"Hell," I remember thinking, "I'd be smiling too if I had that much money and wasn't on my way to Iraq."

A soldier from our unit told me later that he had a conversation with him when he went outside to smoke a cigarette and that he was a real nice guy. I thought, well that's great, a nice little story to tell your grandkids; if you end up surviving the War that is.

What stood out to me about seeing 50 Cent wasn't the fact that I liked his music, honestly, I've never sat and listened to any of it so I can't comment on that. It was the fact that I was thinking about recording an album before I was sent to Iraq.

I went and checked out a studio in Tilton, NH and paid for some recording time before I knew I was being sent overseas. After I found out I was going to Iraq, I went back to the store to try and get my money back. I assumed he would have some compassion for me and let me get a refund. But I was wrong. And this was one of the first times I truly got a distaste for how some people run a business.

The owner of the store told me, "well hey, you might want to try and do some recording before you go, because, you know, you could lose an arm or something."

Jesus Christ, I thought. Was this guy being serious? I just stared blankly at him for a moment thinking, "what the fuck man?"

I left and never ended up recording anything with him. I just figured he was trying to get me to record so he could keep the money. He didn't really give a shit that I was going to War and might lose a limb. But Jesus fuck man.

Still to this day I can't believe that asshole said that to me. The business isn't there anymore, and I can't say that I wonder why.

From Atlanta we went on to Germany, and then Kuwait, before flying into Mosul, Iraq on March 10th. I remember flying over the Atlantic Ocean for the first time and thinking how incredible it was to be up there. It was just mind-blowing.

Since I can remember I have been afraid of the ocean, or more specifically the sharks and other untamed creatures that live there. So, flying over their natural habitat caused my anxiety to get up there just a bit. It wasn't enough for my displeasure to be noticed by any of my fellow soldiers, but it was there.

I kept the irrational fear at bay for now and focused on more pressing matters. I was going to Europe for the first time in my life, but it wouldn't be for long because it was just a quick blip to our real destination. Iraq.

A country we had invaded just a year earlier on the guise that its Dictator was a definite evil to the world, and more specifically, the United States of America, hell bent on using weapons of mass destruction.

Of course, now we know it to be a blatant lie, or more politely, a severely misguided decision with more than plausible ulterior motives. Though it didn't matter to those of us that were going to War then. All we knew, and needed to know, was that we were going to War for our country.

As Rudyard Kipling once wrote, "Ye Thought? Ye are not paid to think."

And that's unfortunately how the Army works at the level of enlistment I was at. But it works.

Someone needs to fight for our Country. History has proven that a nation with a lackluster military is about as likely to stand as long as the life of a pair of Chinese dwarf hamsters.

Of course, having a strong Military doesn't give a country that much more of a chance at posterity, but the probability does increase. Having a strong military gives us the strength to stand against those who want to undermine our values. Even if those values differ from person to person, we must stand as one.

I can't speak for everyone in Baqubah, but I'd like to think we went to War for our fellow Americans. Personally, I was fighting for the guy who wasted his life away at the bar, who spouted off crass liberal ideas and then died alone in a ditch somewhere cold. I was fighting for the idea of choice, and America is still a land of unimaginable choice. Regardless of how corrupt the political system may be, America is still a land of choice.

Chapter 6 Qualia

"Hell isn't other people. Hell is yourself." -Ludwig Wittgenstein

When a crowded city hub clears out in a few minutes, it only means one thing. And it's not a coincidence.

The odds are better of sticking your face in a bucket of crabs and not getting snipped.

The first time it happened in April, I had barely called into the TOC to report the oddness of barren city streets when the first shots rang out. One bounced right over my head. Not nearly as close as when McGuire almost got blasted in the face on OP 2, but still, it shakes your brain up.

But I can't even focus on that right now. I know an attack is coming. I can feel it. But it's so cold. And my Oakley's aren't doing a goddamn thing to help me. The sand burns my skin. It's creeping past my protective gear and really starting to bother me.

Fuck this sand. Fuck it! Christ.

Another beautiful goddamn day on the roof of this goddamn building. Will it ever end? I did the math once. 12-hours a day, 6-days a week. What's that over a one-year period, with no days off?

At least it's quiet today. Great, why did I say that? That's bad luck.

It's always bad luck to say things are quiet.

The first time I said it, hell, even thought it, someone died. Someone always seems to die in this place. Not in easy ways *either. Not in nice ways. Not in your sleep surrounded by loved ones. You're more likely to be surrounded by rubble when you die here.*

And there's only so many cigarettes you can smoke in one day. Literally. I've done it. There is only so much time in a day, only so many cigarettes can be smoked.

Where was... What was I doing? Oh shit! That looks like an ambush! Well fuck me sideways...

Looking back at what led up to the War, I can see how my thoughts back then were very misinformed. Probably because I watched too much cable television.

I knew nothing about the United States involvement with Iraq, or the history of Iraq prior to reading about its years later. I think Noam Chomsky put the idea of our governments misguided venture of war perfectly, when he wrote, "...Saddam Hussein is a 'vengeful despot who has already used chemical and biological weapons on his own citizens,' which is the ultimate horror.

Obviously, such a creature must be destroyed. He poses an enormous threat. He can't be tolerated. So, you bomb him. Impose sanctions.

That's essentially the universal explanation. That justification does have at least one merit: it's very easily tested. You simply must ask, what was the US-British reaction when Saddam Hussein used chemical weapons against his own people? The reaction was that the US and Britain increased support for their favorite monster. They had been supporting Hussein avidly right through his worst crimes; after the gassing, they increased the support. It's not a secret. We can easily discover it." (Iraq Under Siege)

This is based on a talk Chomsky gave on January 30th, 1999 in Cambridge, Massachusetts. And it makes me wonder what my thoughts about the war would have been if I had known it before joining the military.

But then I remember Kipling and the thinking ends.

Knowing what I know now, the whole buildup to what led to the Iraq War seems like a well-placed marketing campaign. Building the country's resentment towards an enemy that had nothing to do with the attacks of September 11th and making us seem so in danger from Iraq we needed to attack them first. No, we must attack them first!

It's concepts like this that I still struggle with today.

On the one hand, America is a beacon of opportunity, in my case at least, and on the other hand, our government seems to be an Empire hell bent on controlling the American people into doing whatever it wills. But none of this mattered to me back in 2004. I was stuck in a situation that I had gladly signed on for, and I don't regret it for a moment.

I think a lot of people feel threatened by knowledge, and at different times in my life this is exactly how I've felt. We are constantly revising who we are as people, and sometimes when we realize we have done things for reasons that were a lie, we don't want to hear it.

It's only the natural human reaction of self-preservation. But just because we may have done something for the wrong reasons, doesn't mean what we did was any less important. It's all part of the human experience. Learning, growing, and understanding.

For example, my perception of the Iraqi people was extremely limited at the onset of the War. All I believed in was serving my country. I never really thought in a larger scale of how the actions of my country affected people in far off lands. But throughout the year in Baqubah, I would start to see things from a completely different perspective.

I would see how the actions of my government seemed absurd at times. I still have complete faith in America though, so don't take this as me bashing a country that I have fought and bled for. And I would be remiss in not saying how grateful I am for the advantages I have been given by being an American citizen and an American soldier. Our military is the cornerstone of our Democracy.

Well, if we overturn Citizens United it will head back to a Democracy, I mean it's really an oligarchy but that's not my point.

My point is that we should always support the men and women who volunteer to fight for our freedom. Always. Regardless of what wars some politicians decide to get us into, we will always need a military. And if you don't think having a strong military is important, you should consider living in another country, say Iraq. And see how not a strong military works out for you.

In doing research for this book, I have learned a lot. I have come to see a lot of the similarities between things that are sometimes hard to grasp at first. One idea is that Saddam Hussein and our government have this in common: They have both visited death and suffering on the people of Iraq.

I was a part of that government, in my opinion. So, I take responsibility for my part in bringing death to Iraq. Specifically, Baqubah. I think the real reason I gave so much away to Iraqis wasn't because I was a decent person. It was because it subconsciously made me feel better for killing so many people. Regardless if they were from Iran, Iraq or Syria. I always felt like the people trying to kill us interacted with us daily, but we just didn't know it.

Sometimes you'd catch a glance that would quickly turn to a fake smile. Other times you knew. You just knew by the look that the person looking at you wanted you dead. And the monsters come when you least expect it. They try to pick you up and throw you right off the goddamn bridge!

Anyway.

This doesn't mean that our government is as inherently evil as Saddam Hussein, or that I am, but it's important to note that our actions can cause the same type of evils if enough thought isn't put into what we do.

Thousands of Iraqi civilians have been killed by American bombs, bullets, and blunders. I heard numerous stories of this from Iraqis that I spoke with during my tour. I also witnessed innocent Iraqis caught in the crossfire during our firefights with insurgents. I think Howard Zinn stated very well what should be thought about with America's constant taste for War in the 21st Century.

He stated, "all we can do is try to convey to the American public the human consequences of our governments repeated use of violence for political and economic gain. When enough of them see and feel what is happening to people just like us – to families, to children – we may see the beginning of a new movement in this country against militarism and war." (pg. 135 in Iraq Under Siege)

I'm not against war. Far from it. I just think the public needs to educate themselves as much as possible about any potential situation which may require it. And even more importantly, that the media reports on these situations with the utmost objectivity.

A fundamental problem in our policies at home and abroad may be the cause of this lack of disconnect. Do we really understand the consequences of our actions? Why are we not doing more to take care of the homeless population in America? What about Veteran Suicide? Is that less of a priority than fixing issues in countries halfway around the world?

I think the answer is complicated. But at a basic level it is an important question to ask ourselves, and I think we need to wake up to this reality.

We need to constantly be questioning the actions of our government.

As Einstein once said, "the important thing is not to stop questioning."

We need to be able to say, no scream, "fuck the government!" as loud and as often as possible.

I also feel we need to love and support it.

This means we need people to volunteer to defend our freedoms and sometimes pay the ultimate price. But questioning the actions of your government and volunteering to fight for it are not contradicting ideas. It's because we have people that willingly fight and die for our country that we can question the actions of the government in the first place. While our government may not be a perfect system, it will stop being an effective one when we stop questioning it.

Ponder this example of a situation involving government decision:

"The US penchant for bombing blots out the government's ability to focus on humanitarian crises – and not just in Iraq. When Hurricane Mitch devastated Central America, leaving tens of thousands dead and more than a million people homeless, there was a desperate need for helicopters to transport people to safety and deliver food and medicine. Mexico supplied sixteen helicopters to Honduras. The United States supplied twelve. At the same time, the Pentagon dispatched a huge armada – helicopters, transport planes, B-52's – to the Middle East. Every cruise missile used to bomb Iraq cost about $1 million, and the Pentagon used more than 300 of them."

At the same time, the Knight Ridder news service reported that the Department of Defense had stopped the distribution of blankets to homeless programs around the country. The Senate Armed Services Committee had not approved the appropriation. According to the news dispatch, "The committee said the $3.5 million annual cost [of the blanket program] diverted money from weapons." Thus, our weapons kill people abroad, while in this country homeless people freeze." (pg. 134-135 Iraq Under Siege)

My point here isn't that America is an evil Empire hell bent on only supporting the needs of the government to self-perpetuate itself. Although under the leadership of some presidential administrations that argument can be made. America is still a land of choice, and we the public need to wake up its collective unconscious and be willing to debate and recognize our mistakes so that we can improve our future and the future of everyone on this planet with an equal amount of passion.

As I stated earlier, I'm also not one of the people who think that War is never necessary. That we should all hold hands and skip around the world smiling and singing... As John Stuart Mill once said, "War is an ugly thing but not the ugliest of things. The decayed and degraded state of mind that thinks nothing is worth fighting for is far worse."

Unfortunately, there are evils in the world that need to be destroyed.

Take the current situation with ISIS in the Middle East. Over ten years after the initial invasion of Iraq, there are groups like this that are murdering thousands of people. They are taking their severely misguided, and more to the point, flat out evil ideas across the globe. An example is the recent attacks on Charlie Hebdo in Paris, France.

This type of evil needs to be dealt with and I am all for the use of force.

In fact, I would gladly sign up again to fight them face-to-face if I could. The rage I feel about the death of the journalist James Foley is hard to hold back at times. I don't think we responded strongly enough about that horrible act of cowardice by ISIS.

I also don't agree with some people, that this evil can be dealt with by a diplomatic solution.

To quote Karl Popper, a great philosophical mind of the last generation, "If we extend unlimited tolerance even to those who are intolerant, then the tolerant will be destroyed, and tolerance with them."

I think it perfectly sums up the situation with ISIS. They are an extremely hate-filled group that no amount of reasoning with can persuade. And we need to deal with this problem before it starts to visit us on our homeland, causing another September 11th of even greater catastrophe.

The type of force we use however is a matter of opinion. And I'm of the opinion that recklessly dropping bombs on an uncertain target is not good practice.

I am for boots on the ground to take out the enemies of America head on. Politicians don't like to do this for obvious reasons, but it's necessary. And no soldier that has ever fought and died for America has ever died in vain. Fighting for America means fighting for the overall safety and survival of our nation. I would never advocate for the use of people to be put in situations that I myself have not been in. I speak as a veteran, and because of this, I stand by my decisions about this matter.

Some things are worth dying for. It's that simple.

Chapter 7 Anxiety

A direct cause of trauma and the solution to healing.

"The oldest and strongest emotion of mankind is fear, and the oldest and strongest kind of fear is fear of the unknown." – H.P. Lovecraft

Every time we kick a door in, I'm sure it'll be the last time.

It's one of the few instances at War where I'm glad I'm wrong. Those thoughts though. Goddamn those thoughts. Damn them straight to fucking hell.

You know, there was a time when all I could think about was happy things. Not puppies and sunflowers kind of happy but, close enough. Now I'm outfitted to take down a city block by myself and unless you're a complete fucking sociopath that feeds off other people's misery, how could you possibly enjoy this?

"Oh, I know how." Says the voice that always comes when I least want to hear it. "You enjoy it. You fucking crave it."

No, I don't.

"But you do. You do enjoy it. It's okay to laugh. It's okay to feel like god. There's nothing wrong with it. You're good at it. Just relax. But not too much because I'll kill you. You may be safe for now, but I will get you. The Monsters always get you in the end, and I'm the biggest and baddest motherfucking monster of them all..."

I stumbled on the topic of anxiety today at Baldface Books in Dover, NH. I was explaining to the owner of the bookstore how I had recently told one of my close friends that I was completely sober. Not even pot? My friend replied. What about pills? Nothing?

I responded no, nothing. Just good old-fashioned sobriety.

He posed the question: Well how do you deal with the anxiety? And I knew exactly what he was talking about because it's the exact reason I used as an excuse to continue drinking and using drugs for the last decade. It's the reason most people give when they are asked why they use drugs or alcohol.

Unfortunately for me, and all the other veterans that suffer from extreme anxiety, PTSD transforms it, into another beast altogether; a debilitating mind game of self-torture where you play dual roles as dungeon master and the accused.

This led me into my discussion with Clyde, the owner of the aforementioned bookstore, about the nature of anxiety. We all have it. In one form or another. Sigmund Freud believed that anxiety is the basis of all neurosis. But regardless of any psychoanalytical ideas, anxiety usually starts with a simple thought.

Clyde went into an example of a perfectly rational and common way anxiety can come about, and that most people in America undoubtedly think about on occasion. He stated, "For instance, say I'm on my way to work, and suddenly the thought comes into my head. What if my car breaks down? What am I going to do? How am I going to get to work? How am I going to pay for the unknown costs?"

And this leads to anxiety about the issue itself, which all starts with a single thought.

But how do we control these thoughts or impulses which seem so rational and are so ingrained in our human nature?

It's a difficult question to answer. Sometimes it's easy to explain in theory, but in practice it's an entirely different beast. So, this led me to think about how anxiety effects veterans and the central role it plays in suicide. The more I think about it, the more I realize that it was anxiety that caused me to make every poor choice regarding my recovery from War.

But what caused this anxiety?

The answer is trauma.

And that leads me back to the conclusion that the more knowledge given to soldiers before they experience trauma, the better they will be at handling it.

What else can cause anxiety though? And what does that answer have to do with trauma? I think the answer is the unknown. But what does the unknown have to do with trauma since the trauma isn't unknown, the person was present when the trauma occurred, or it couldn't be considered trauma at all?

The unknown has to do with the uncertainty in knowing whether that trauma, or something similar, will happen again. To better understand this idea, we must look at what trauma is.

Trauma is defined as a deeply distressing or disturbing experience. But I don't think that definition is descriptive enough. Trauma demoralizes your entire being to the core. It breaks it down so that the fundamental building blocks that have been painstakingly placed there by your psyche become loose and the mind has nothing left to stand on. It's like being born again but in an even more frightening world and fully aware that the world is a terrible place. And that's all you see.

It's this act of awareness that brings in the idea of the unknown. It's a sharp awakening to the fact that we don't know how certain things really are. That's the trauma.

So, trauma is experiencing the unknown. It would only make sense that if this is the case, then knowledge is the key to curbing the longevity of mental pain a person gets from a traumatic event. Hence, knowledge better prepares a person to deal with trauma, or any other subject or illness for that matter.

Only when we truly understand a problem can, we start to deal with it. So, the logical next step to help stop Veteran Suicide in the future is to better prepare the soldiers who are in boot camp now by informing them about trauma. This doesn't have to be a specifics-oriented type of knowledge, but a broad-based lesson on how a human reacts to traumatic events. Recruits learn how to react to chest wounds and blown up body parts, so why not learn how to bandage up and treat the mind?

How do we help soldiers who are dealing with PTSD now?

That's a bit more complicated. But maybe it isn't. It's certainly more mentally taxing because the veteran must learn about trauma after experiencing it, which causes them to associate the horrible things they feel about the situation to the actual learning about trauma itself. This poses a problem. And its why many veterans choose drugs or alcohol, so they don't have to think about the trauma they experienced.

But there is a better way.

It can't be forced though. The individual must *want* to be able to deal with what happened to them.

You can't force knowledge on somebody. They must have an actual interest in it. A key component in having an actual interest in staying sober is living in a happy environment. It's amazing how drugs and alcohol seem less urgent when your life isn't in pandemonium. Physical addiction is a hell of a thing. A hell of a fucking thing. But the mental side of addiction is the key cog to unraveling its grip.

Chapter 8 The Iraqis

"You've got to write badly. If you write badly at least you've got something to rewrite. If you're scared to write badly, then you've got nothing." -Tony Grisoni

The first time I tripped out in Iraq, I chugged two bottles of NyQuil and sat outside in the dark by a small pond located in Saddam Hussain's massive compound in Tikrit. Well, it was 2004 so it used to belong to him.

We hadn't gotten to Baqubah yet, and so far, every place we stopped, Mosul and now here, it seemed like I might be in for a very uneventful tour. This was early February 2004.

Normally it takes a solid hour to start robo-tripping from NyQuil, but if you chug two bottles you are going to feel drunk and full immediately. I waited well past when everyone else went to sleep. Silently chugged the stuff in my sleeping bag laying on the floor of one of the massive buildings. I waited with anticipation for the night to come, but it hit faster than ever before, and after 15 agonizing minutes, I felt like I was secretly transforming into some sort of monster.

I had no idea of the monster I was to become. I remember getting up and making my way outside when I sat down by a small pond right beside the building, we temporarily called home. I remember the sky seemed different than any sky I'd ever seen. It was as if someone changed the battery in the flashlight behind the blanket with holes punched in it. The sky was magnificent. I just sat there in awe marveling at my current situation when our Platoon Sgt St. Cyr came out and immediately started talking to me. The only thing I can remember next is telling him at some point how comforting it was being able to see Orion's belt because I use to look at it often outside my bedroom window in Dixfield as a child, from the comfort of my own bed.

During the hottest parts of the Iraqi summer, the days in Baqubah would sometimes pass without notice. Besides the heat that would boil your brain like a well heated cup of clam chowder; some days were quite uneventful. Of course, IED's were a daily occurrence, but at the police station, for a few short weeks during the excruciating summer heat, we weren't hit with the normal bombardment of RPG and mortar rounds.

Sure, there would be the occasional sniper round that lodged near a soldier's head. Sergeant Mark McGuire can attest to that shit. But other than that, it was like a time-lapse video of a bustling city like any other, except for the dirt, the sun, and the occasional passerby who would bend down mid-walk and casually take a shit on the side of the street.

Crowds of people would walk up and down the street during the day. The busy city streets would be filled with cars and just as often, with a man herding a few dozen sheep. It would be like seeing a farmer walk his herd through the center of Boston on a busy Friday afternoon. Except in Iraq, Fridays were like American Sundays. So, like a busy Wednesday afternoon in the streets of Cambridge.

Vehicle safety wasn't something the Iraqis really seemed to care about either. Trucks would be carrying rebar down the streets and the rebar would be twice as long as the truck carrying it. Sparks would slap up and over the car behind it, which didn't seem to sense any danger at all and would still honk their horn at the truck to speed up. Horns seemed to be a delight to the drivers in Baqubah. They would bark back and forth at each other like a coordinated symphony that had an audience hanging on the edge of its seat. Except the audience was just the soldiers standing on rooftops throughout the city, watching the absurdity of humanity through their unique vantage point.

Days in Baqubah were like a scene out of *Ground Hogs Day* except sprinkle in a touch of *Mad Max* to complete the picture. The movie *Mad Max* was my first thought when we arrived in Baqubah. My first fucking thought. Driving around the trash strewn streets, all you could see was garbage and raw sewage on every scrap of roadway throughout the city.

It seemed like an apocalyptic wasteland where oil would be the only viable currency. And I'm not going to tell you anything about the time some raw sewage splashed into my open mouth during a mounted patrol in Tahrir. I think the last sentence tells you everything you need to know about that. And to say being in Iraq was a culture shock is a complete understatement.

I knew that I would be constantly offending people with my American ways, and that ended up being true. Right up until the day I left. But I also made some amazing Iraqi friends along the way. It was one strange trip, and, in the end, we are all human, so even with the language barrier, if you sit next to someone long enough, you are bound to find common ground.

That's how I became friends with most of the Iraqi Police Officers and Iraqi Interpreters. Besides the rooftop OP's, two of the OP's also had an Iraqi police officer or two on guard as well. For the first few months it was just a lot of hand gesturing and nodding "yes" by both parties when I'm sure neither one of us knew anything the other one was saying. Although some of the Iraqis knew a lot more English than they led us to believe, those cheeky bastards. I would do the same thing if I were them. It was an incredibly smart strategy.

But a smile... everyone recognizes a genuine smile regardless of language or culture. And the Iraqi people loved to smile. It didn't seem like anything could keep them down for too long. It was an endearing characteristic of their culture. Something that most of us in the United States take for granted. The ability to laugh and enjoy life no matter what the circumstances are. *I also made quite a few Iraqi friends by having them buy me alcohol. Whiskey. Lebanese whiskey. A bottle cost maybe $2 and I would give them $20 a pop. One of the reasons why I liked to overpay was to help ensure my safety.*

That might not make sense at first, but if someone is being paid handsomely by a U.S. Soldier for something, they are far less likely to kill them. I also donated money for an Iraqi police officer's daughter's hospital operation by giving him $100. I remember I was on OP1 when I saw him running and I had never seen this guy run before. He stopped looked up, and I dropped money down I had for him. He thanked me and ran off. Other soldiers also helped by giving food or other necessities when they could.

Afterall, we didn't live on a nice cozy base. We lived with the Iraqi people, at least the ones who had decided to risk their own lives by working with us. Maintaining a positive relationship with our Iraqi colleagues always stayed towards the forefront of my thoughts.

Another reason I overpaid for everything I bought from my Iraqi counterparts was that I genuinely felt bad for what they were going through.

I'm not trying to make myself out to be a Saint. I'm just saying it was hard to not notice how awful many Iraqis had it. Here were people who had to suffer innumerable horrors under Saddam Hussein and although they were now free of him, they still had to eat.

Unemployment was a huge issue for them obviously. In turn it must have been extremely difficult to earn a living to feed their families. That's not Quantum Physics or String Theory.

Their economy wasn't booming. The Iraqi Dinar was rendered worthless after the invasion.

It was a hard concept to try and grasp at the time. Because while I was wrestling with questions like this, I still had to worry about my fellow soldiers and myself twenty-four hours a day. But the Iraqi men that lined up to get jobs as police officers and members of the Iraqi army, in the face of the dangers that came with it, was a testament to how desperate they were to make a living.

Not all were excited to serve their country as a police officer or member of the army, but through talking with many of them, a lot did just want to serve their homeland in one way or another.

I gave what I could, when I could. It may have not been a lot, and it surely wasn't my responsibility to provide every Iraqi enough money to feed their family, but isn't that what humans are supposed to do for one another? Genuinely care? I think so.

I'm not saying I went around all the time like Mother Theresa, showing compassion to every Iraqi I came across, because that is far from the truth. I lost my shit on some Iraqi civilians quite a few times during the War.

On one occasion there was a line of over a hundred Iraqis trying to get into the police station to file grievances, or conduct other types of business, and they were not listening very well to our instructions. For obvious reasons. They all didn't know English and I sure as fuck didn't know Arabic well enough. The Iraqi police were talking to them and trying to get them to not push and force themselves in, but the message wasn't getting through.

It was like a nearby high school just ended for the day and all the students were now lined up to buy tickets to a Spose concert and were so excited that common courtesy went right out the fucking window. PDANK XMAS 7 is going to be the most insane show in Maine music history, and you can still buy tickets for it. How cool is that? It's some Dr. Who shit.

So, I started to feel completely overwhelmed by the number of people trying to gain access to the police station, and there was only one other U.S. soldier stationed with me to deal with it. So, I decided to pull my 9mm out, point it straight up in the air, and yell, get the fuck back. (I may have pointed it directly at the face of the first Iraqi in front of me.)

Everyone calmed down after that.

I'm not saying I dealt with it in the best way. I just dealt with the extremely stressful situation the only way I could think of. I wasn't trained for that shit. I may have been given the MOS of 31B and trained for a few weeks to cover the basics, but I was in no way trained extensively enough to deal with this shit.

What I kept thinking about was the safety of everyone inside the building. What if someone had a bomb on them? What if some of them had weapons and were trying to get in without being checked properly? That's why I pulled my handgun out.

With better training, that situation may have been handled better. But I didn't get any training like that at Ft. Dix. I'll elaborate more about Ft. Dix and the army's infinite wisdom in a little bit.

I was just listening to a conversation that Ali and Jack had with me on one of the tapes from Iraq and I came across an interesting conversation, at least to me.

We were talking about how they didn't like to use toilets. The two Iraqi translators were profoundly proud of the fact they didn't use them and gave me numerous examples of why it is better to squat and take a shit instead of using a goddamn toilet. I found this a little interesting because communal facilities were developed in ancient Mesopotamia over 4,400 years ago, extremely close to the spot they were standing on in an Ancient Palace at Eshnunna on the Diyala River in Iraq around 2,300 B.C.

"A palace at Eshnunna, on the Diyala River, in Iraq, dating to around 2300 B.C., had six toilets with raised seats of baked brick set in a row. These were connected to bitumen-lined drains leading into a brick sewer three feet deep. Each of the lavatories had a large water vessel placed next to it, containing a pottery dipper that was used to the flush the toilet after use." (Ancient Inventions pg. 442 By Peter James and Nick Thorpe).

So, what caused the people living in this exact spot over 4,000 years later to think that something their ancestors used and had a help in inventing, was now something to not be used? Most likely the loss of knowledge due to incredible controlling despots who have been ruling the area for centuries.

The overall mood of the Iraqi people usually seemed optimistic and it didn't make sense to me until I had a talk with an Iraqi friend of mine who told me that a lot of people in Iraq just live for today. They don't worry about what will happen in the future. Or what happened yesterday. They just enjoy the moment.

This seemed like an extremely shortsighted concept to me back then. But it was brilliant.

And as I listen to the tapes of Ali describing this, I sound like an asshole completely missing the point. But I understood the mentality of it. It was kind of like a "well fuck it" attitude, which is an oversimplification of the idea, but you get my point.

It's also funny to me now that I look back on my own life, because that's the exact same attitude I would take while my life was falling apart after my second divorce. It's a natural human reaction to a terrible situation. And I think above everything else that it gets lost somewhere along the lines in our everyday lives.

The simple fact that we are all human, and we all make mistakes.

Sometimes we lose sight of that and try hurt others because we think they don't care or don't deserve this or that. But we are all just trying to make it through another day, and we need to remember that. We need to remember that and move forward. We also need to remember that there are evil people in the world; people that harm others emotionally and physically, for their own benefit.

I felt the shields in the turrets of the Humvees they had us put up at one point during the tour made it harder for me to do any damage to the evil fuckers of the world. It made me feel less safe doing my job because it cut down my visibility and I had to completely stand up in the vehicle to see over them properly. Which made me feel like even more of a target.

And besides, we looked goddamn menacing when we were in the turret *without* the shields. It looked fucking badass.

I think this played a psychological role on the enemy. In as much as we looked like a hard target (one that was ready and looking for a fight to be in) as opposed to a soft target (one that looked unready to fight). I always thought this might have been a reason we weren't attacked as often by IED's. I'm not discounting luck. Luck was my battle buddy. We had a reputation for fighting back when we were attacked and fighting back ferociously.

If I was the enemy, I wouldn't attack a group of soldiers that were known to fuck shit up at the first sign of trouble and keep it up until the threat was gone. We proved this to our enemy in the first few months of our tour. We would prove time and time again that we were not going to roll over for the enemy and hide in our building, which wouldn't have been safe at all if the walls had been breached, which is exactly what the insurgents were trying to do on April, 9th 2004 for example.

We had even been told at one point in time to get ready to evacuate the police station if need be. But fuck that! We were holding that bitch; it was our home. And maybe that's a very American idea. To be so far from home, and in a country, we invaded but think only after a short time living there, the spot we were occupying was our home. But it was.

We ate, slept, laughed, joked, and lived our daily lives, such as they were, in that decrepit old brick building. And when someone decided to shoot at us, I took it very personally. I held the same rage I might hold if someone was shooting at me while I was sitting on my front porch back in the United States. Afterall, I didn't start this War. I was just doing my job in that moment of time. What did I personally ever do to anyone trying to kill me? I never just opened fire on unsuspecting Iraqis.

I did offend quite a few Iraqis with my ignorance of their culture, but that was not on purpose, and not an offense that warranted me to be killed. So, every time we were attacked in Baqubah I took it as an intolerance of the highest order.

Thinking in this way also made it easy for me to pull the trigger on the enemy. If you find yourself in a situation where you are protecting your home from an intruder who is trying to kill you with RPG's and AK-47's, it's not so hard to find yourself pulling the trigger of a weapon aimed at those trying to kill you.

We couldn't call 911. We were our own 911. And Baqubah was our home.

Now it's easy to say, 'but it wasn't your home, you were an invading force, occupying a country thousands of miles from home.' Yes, that may be true. But the soldier can't think like that if he wants to survive.

The realities of why we were there, and the politics of how we came to be there were dangerous ideas to us. And they are dangerous ideas for any solider currently on the frontlines of a War to ponder.

Too much thinking about the how's and why's can get you killed.

We always had a protection force watching the building from the roof and front gate along with a rover who patrolled around the complex at different timed intervals. So, there was a sense of comfort in knowing that the enemy couldn't just waltz in and kill us all in our sleep. But it wasn't that much of a comfort. Because if that did happen, if an Iraqi police officer decided to bring in an IED on his person and blow up the building, there wasn't a damn thing we could do about it.

We did live in constant fear of death at any moment. Literally. It wouldn't have been that hard at all for someone to do. In fact, a short while after we left the building something like that did happen. Someone came in and detonated a bomb in the small cafeteria area in the back of the compound. (I need to ask people about this event...)

I'd like to think that all the fraternizing I did with the Iraqis helped them see I was human, and I was in fact trying to help them out. I did this on a constant basis, mostly because I found living with another culture so fascinating, and another because of my aforesaid statement, which is just self-preservation when it comes right down to it.

Building relations with the people you work with forms trust and comradery as well. Most of the Iraqis I saw daily went home most nights, which meant they were exposed to all sorts of danger that I wasn't. It also meant they could be an insurgent if they so choose to be. There was no need for me to give them any more reason to hate American Soldiers than the insurgent propaganda machine was already putting in as many heads as possible – that we were evil Americans only there for the oil.

I got this last statement from an Iraqi Interpreter named Ali when I asked him what Iraqis thought about Americans before we came to their country. And then I asked him what he thought about us after we came here and his reply was, "monsters."

I was a little shocked at first, but then I asked him to go on because I was intrigued at what he was saying. Now you must understand that I built up a good friendship with Ali over the course of months. We shared hypothetical whiskey more than a few times and joked around every time we saw each other. I was glad to hear, first off, that he felt safe enough to say something like that to a fully armed soldier that had taken over his beloved city, and second off, because he had said it so honestly.

When he began to explain what he meant he started with this:

"You guys are like people from the moon, and you come down with all your technology that we had never seen before."

And then it started to dawn on me...

"You mean aliens?"

"Yes!"

He hadn't meant "monsters" in our sense of the word at all. He meant aliens. It's amazing how language can be so easily mistranslated and misinterpreted.

Chapter 9 Yasser and Jack

"True friendship comes when silence between two people is comfortable." –Dave Tyson Gentry

One of my closest Iraqi friends was named Yasser. He was a tough son of a bitch and one of the few Iraqi police officers who would run towards a firefight instead of away from it. It was a common theme when we first arrived in Baqubah, to see the Iraqis we were supposed to be fighting with run in the opposite direction of any enemy contact.

A mortar attack would take place and then the Iraqis would turn into Olympic track stars. But not Yasser. He seemed to revel in it. He was proud of his country. Proud of his job. And he did it well. We spent a lot of time telling each other jokes and laughing about the stupid shit we encountered every day.

One day while working the front gate an old man came up to me showing an I.D. that was clearly not him. And all he was saying that I could understand was that he was a police officer, this was his I.D., and he wanted to get into the compound. Recognizing that the man on the I.D. wasn't the guy in front of me, I proceeded to check him for weapons and handcuffed him with zip-ties, our standard handcuffs in Iraq, and led him into the jail for questioning.

The whole time Yasser was watching this exchange he just had a huge smile on his face. I didn't pay it much attention because I was focused on trying to keep someone out of our building that was obviously trying to get in under false pretenses. Or so I thought.

What really happened was the guy was the father of an Iraqi police officer that had left his I.D. at home and this gentleman was trying to return it to his son because he was obviously worried about his boy, and knew he would need it for his own safety. Yasser heard and saw the whole exchange but just decided to let me arrest the guy anyway.

It was good entertainment. After I dropped the guy off in jail, Yasser explained to me what had really happened and I just looked at him like, 'Jesus man, I bet you enjoyed every second of that didn't you?'

The older gentleman was immediately released of course and shook my hand as he left the compound, smiling the whole time. From that point on, anytime an older Iraqi approached the front gate the Iraqis would jokingly warn them that they should be careful because I was probably going to arrest them.

That joke never got old and it made me laugh every time. I was just doing my job when I had the old guy arrested, and the good fun the Iraqis were having at my expense brought us all closer together.

The day before I left Baqubah for good I gave Yasser the K-bar fighting knife I had kept on the front of my armor for the entire tour. His friendship meant that much to me, and I felt like I wanted to do whatever I could to help keep him safe after I left. Of course, I couldn't really do anything about that, but I cared for the guy.

Just before I left, he came up to me and gave me a picture of himself with some Arabic writing on the back. And it wasn't until ten years later that I would find the picture again and get the message he had handwritten on the back translated. It simply said, "To Marshall, Yasser gives this gift to Marshall. Your brother, Yasser."

That makes me smile. I had come to his country as an invading force, yet he considered me his brother – his friend. And I'd like to think that regardless of how the war may have started, we left some Iraqi people with the knowledge that there are people out there who really do care about others; regardless of who or where you are in life, genuine compassion is still alive and well.

Then there was an Iraqi Translator named Jack that was known to drink large amounts of alcohol at all times. I really liked him. He seemed like he always had a constant hangover and was constantly cursing the sun.

After he had a few shots of whiskey one night I asked him if he wanted to hypothetically smoke some pot I had from the United States. He was hesitant at first and told me he had never tried it. I didn't really believe him, but he agreed to smoke some, so we went into his room on the first floor of the police station and lit up.

We passed the joint around for a few minutes, just chilled, and the conversation started to slow down a bit, as they tend to do at times when smoking pot. He started to get a look of surprise which slowly came over him. Then he looked me in the eyes, the best he could at that moment, put one hand in front of his face with his palm facing him and pulled down in a few repetitive motions like he was pulling an invisible string from his nose to his heart.

I was a little confused at what the hell he was doing until he said, as he made the hand motion, "I feel it here. I feel it. Here. Am I supposed to feel it here? I feel it. Here" Motioning over his face and heart.

I started belly laughing so hard at this honest assessment of a first-time marijuana user and realized he probably hadn't ever smoked weed before. And if he had, it wasn't anything this good. It was always a sweet reprieve occasionally tasting my home state of Maine.

Chapter 10 Field Tremors

"I decline to accept the end of man. It is easy enough to say that man is immortal simply because he will endure, that when the last ding-dong of doom has changed and faded from the last worthless rock hanging tide less in the last red and dying evening, that even then there will still be one more sound: that of his puny, inexhaustible voice still talking." Nobel Laureate William Faulkner expresses his heartfelt belief that, "Man will not merely endure: He will prevail."

Even though It may seem like I was reckless in my drug use, I want to make the case for reason and logic still having a center role in my life, especially when it comes to drugs. I always took dosage very seriously. You must be precise. There was one other soldier who I had serious discussions with about what drugs we should or should not perhaps have on hand at the police station.

It's a common misconception that people who use drugs to reach higher levels of consciousness or help curb pain in unwanted circumstances are mindless addicts. That usually ends up being the case, but it is not how it all began for me.

Yes, we drank, but rarely, and the only drug we used was marijuana, which is, as I stated earlier, safer than aspirin. But during this conversation we were pondering the idea of bringing cocaine to the war front. Everything in my soul screamed, "no!" We came to the unanimous decision we already had enough demons, literal and figurative, daily in Baqubah. Having that monkey on our back wouldn't have been good for anyone.

While the marijuana we smoked helped relax us and cope with the daily horror, it didn't have any negative effects on the soldiers around us. Cocaine use would have put other soldiers in danger. As fucked up as my morals are, that's just a line I was not willing to cross.

I tried to write as often as I could in Iraq. At first, I wrote almost daily. But after my first few times in combat, my attitude towards writing shifted.

I stopped writing. I stopped logging down what I felt and thought during the day and only a sporadic amount of writing would be done for the rest of the tour.

I felt at the time that there wasn't a point in it. I was so disillusioned with life and the horrors of war that I didn't think anything mattered anymore. I realize now that I was suffering from PTSD early in the tour. Because immediately after my first few experiences in combat, which would go into the dozens by the end of my tour, I had a sense of impending doom fall over me. Which is the reason I stopped writing.

I stopped believing in anything. I started to run on autopilot emotionally. If you could even say I had any emotions at all... I shut down that human part of me and began joking about awful things to cope with the horror.

During one mission where we had to cordon off an area after an IED had killed dozens of Iraqis, there was an arm on the ground that looked like it was still twitching. To this day I'm not sure if the arm was moving or not, but in my mind, I saw it waving. So, I said to my sergeant, "hey sarge, look, that guy is waving at you."

He looked over and saw the lifeless limb just lying next to the vehicle and said, "Jesus Marshall, what the fuck?"

I just laughed and pressed on with my duties. Days turned into weeks. And all the while we joked and laughed about horrible things.

It never dawned on me that I was already dealing with the effects of PTSD. I had shut down the emotions inside of me. That part of me that was human seemed to be dying. And at some points I thought it would never come back.

Chapter 11 A Mystic Bond

"The mystic bond of brotherhood makes all men one." –Thomas Carlyle

At least a dozen rounds sunk into his body before I could even comprehend the fact that we had killed him. Karl Schumaker was in the turret behind me, and he put a few holes in him as well. It wasn't the first time though; I think this was number six. Well maybe it was seven. It's hard to tell when they take the bodies away before we can get to them.

A patrol had been hit on RPG ally and we happened to be on QRF. That meant it was our job to take the wounded to Warhorse for treatment. We happened to come under fire while traveling 45 mph north towards the base. I got out of the kill-zone as quickly as I could and then popped up out of the Humvee just as fast, spun my turret, locked it and looked down the site of my M249 SAW. I didn't even have to aim because the enemy was happily waiting for me. When I think back to it, he always smiles. They always seem to smile.

About a week later someone working in the TOC would tell me an older couple came in asking why their son had been killed by Mufrek Circle. He wasn't an insurgent they professed; he was a good kid.

Well, your good kid was holding an AK-47 about 75 yards from where my Humvee was getting peppered with bullets. And he was in the same direction the bullets were coming from. You do the math. I must make quick decisions. Either he played a part in trying to kill me and my Brothers or he has the world's shittiest luck. Goddamn War.

Jameson Holmes. I first started to talk more often with him once we got settled into Baqubah. He was always entertaining and had so many goddamn stories about his life back home. They were always a great escape.

We were assigned to the same Humvee but had one too many men on our team, so we took turns in the turret for missions to give each other a rest. It just happened to be his day in the turret when he ended up being hit with an IED.

I remember standing outside of the building at the police station when I heard an extremely loud explosion in the distance. It was almost like a "poof" in time. I thought to myself about our guys who were currently in that direction at the time on a mission. I dismissed it and carried on. But not long after we got word that our guys had been hit. And when we asked who it was, somebody said, "some black guy from the New Hampshire unit."

We didn't have any black guys in our unit, so we all immediately assumed the worst. That he had been hit so badly his body was charred.

Thankfully that wasn't the case. Those of us still at the police station didn't know that at the time. He did however have one hell of a coating of debris all over him that did make him look like a different ethnicity.

They pulled back into the police station before taking him to the nearest base and I remember not wanting to go over to him because at this point in time I thought he was most likely dead, and I wasn't sure how I would react to that. I stayed away and then got in another turret as we mounted up to bring him over to get medical care at FOB Warhorse.

He ended up making it but had a large amount of shrapnel peppered throughout his body. I remember talking to him at one point not long after, while he was in the States, and he was contemplating trying to come back over and rejoin us. I remember berating him, telling him that if he did, I would be extremely upset with him.

He got his ticket home, and he earned it. If he pushed and fought to come back, I *would* have been extremely upset with him. This was very selfish of me. But I didn't want to see a friend of mine who had already been blown up and gone through hell and back, to come back to hell.

This was a guy who fought just as hard as the toughest of us. He held OP 2 down like a maniac on April 9th, standing clear of cover he showered the enemy with rounds from his M249 SAW and kept those fuckers from taking that part of the police station. This was a man who went out on a mission and got wounded from an IED and god damnit he deserved to not come back.

Chapter 12 Insanity, Reality or Both?'

"Insanity—a perfectly rational adjustment to an insane world." –R.D. Laing

Here's the most beneficial way I've ever heard PTSD described…

Let's say you're watching a movie and right in the middle of it another movie starts playing in the middle of the screen. Sometimes it grows, taking over the whole TV. It's so intrusive your eyes become focused on the unwanted images being blasted. Sometimes you barely notice it. But it's always there. Shrinking, growing, spinning, and you have no idea how to control it. Not yet.

And now I'm going to talk about something that most soldiers will never talk about. And it's not easy for me to bring these things up. But I think it's important so that we can better understand the tragedies of war and help the soldiers of the future. To do this we have to look inside the psyche of a soldier. It's worth it to understand the ways humans react in the face of constant traumatic events.

Why is it worth it? So that we can better understand the problems facing us as a society.

One of these problems is Veteran Suicide and to better face this issue we must first look at the root cause. A good start is by looking into the mind of a soldier when the trauma was experienced. As we step into this unknown, it's important to keep an open mind.

We went on a mission to find some guy's head.

Let that sink in for a moment.

That was the basis for our mission that night. To go out in the darkness that was Baqubah and find a human head.

We ended up finding it at the nearby hospital and a bunch of people had their picture taken with it. I didn't. But I can remember thinking to myself whether I wanted to or not. And that's a hell of thing. Trying to decide if it's okay or not to take a picture of yourself holding up a dead guy's head.

Would I smile? Would I have a stone-cold face? Is it even a good idea at all? Hell no. But I understand why people did it. Christ I even thought about doing it myself!

War has a way of wearing down the human in you. It changes you forever, but it doesn't have to change you forever in a negative way. At first that's all I saw, and that's all I focused on. This was a traumatic event for me. One of many. It made me feel inhuman. Disconnected.

At the time I laughed and joked with the other soldiers around me. We didn't know our humor was the way we were coping with trauma. Hell, we didn't even know what we were experiencing was trauma, because we had grown so accustomed to it. To death. To hell. To everything that lives on the fucked upside of humanity.

But maybe there's a way we can better prepare soldiers to process and deal with these types of events. Some fucked up shit happens in war.

Some. Fuckcd. Up. Shit.

I think if soldiers understand that better, they will be able to not only handle traumatic events better, but they will be able to deal with and understand them better once they are out of uniform.

Not every soldier is interested in history before they join the military. Sure, it's safe to say that almost all have watched movies about War. But that hardly qualifies a person to be ready to understand the true scope of the situation. We watch movies, especially when we are young, as mere entertainment. And when you're watching a movie for entertainment purposes, you hardly retain any of the concepts that may be in the film.

Yes, you process them, and can say, 'wow, that's some horrible shit.' But you don't fully understand the true horror that is front of you. At least I didn't. Not until I experienced it.

Being in the presence of death is far different than watching a reenactment. But if I had taken numerous classes about trauma and the real effects of war during boot camp or at some point before going to War, I might have been better prepared to understand it.

Created by Aaron Lee Marshall
Illustrated by Jeff Wheeler

The driver was warned multiple times, we followed every procedure at the time. But sometimes training plus luck arent enough. Maybe he was telling a joke to his dog as one of his wives and daughters rode in the cold, dirty bed of the truck.

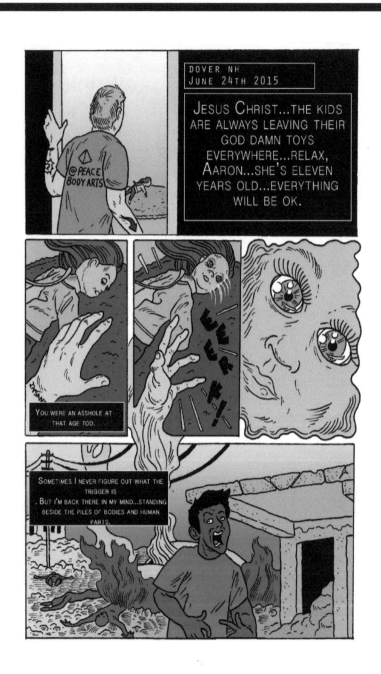

123

I DON'T EVEN KNOW WHY I TOOK THE TIME TO TAP OUT THAT JOINT.

I SUPPOSE IT'S BECAUSE IT'S THE ONLY THING KEEPING ME FROM LOSING MY GOD DAMN MIND.

ALRIGHT, POINT OF ORIGIN IS CONFIRMED. I ACTUALLY CAN'T BELIEVE I JUST SAW THAT SHIT. CONTACT ON OP4.

IF I DON'T RETURN FIRE INTO THE DARKNESS OF THE CITY, THEY'LL KEEP SHOOTING, AND THEN THEY'LL START TO ADD MORTARS. THE NIGHTS ADD ON. RPG'S PUNCH US DAILY AND THEN WEEKLY AS THE GRIND BEGAN TO TAKE ITS TOLL.

The world is like a ride at an amusement park, and when you choose to go on it, you think its real cause that's how powerful our minds are.

And the ride goes up and down and round and round. It has thrills and chills and it's very brightly colored and it's very loud and its fun...

For awhile.

Some people have been on the ride for a long time, and they begin to question: "Is this real or is this just a ride?"

And other people have remembered, and they come back to us, they say, "Hey, don't worry, don't be afraid, EVER, because THIS is just a ride."

BAQUBAH COMICS Issue #2 Mind Fuxk

Created by Aaron Lee Marshall
Illustrated by Jeff Wheeler

WE WERE OFTEN SENT OUT TO RETRIEVE THE DEAD.

SOMETIMES WE WERE PUT IN SITUTATIONS WE COULD HAVE NEVER PREPARED FOR. THERE ARE NO COURSES IN THE ARMY THAT TEACH YOU HOW TO STUFF A BODY INTO THE TRUNK OF A NEARLY FULL HUMVEE. AND, MORE IMPORTANTLY, HOW TO DEAL WITH IT PSYCHOLOGICALLY AFTER.

NOISES THAT LEAVE THE FRESHLY DECEASED DO NOT NET TO BE DESCRIBED.

DON'T USE YOUR IMAGINATION

132

ON THIS PARTICULAR DAY WE SET OUT TO RETRIEVE THE FIRST BODY OF THE SHIFT. I CAN STILL TASTE THE SAND. I CAN ALWAYS TASTE SAND WHEN WORKING ON THIS SHIT. FEEL THE GRIT POP BETWEEN MY TEETH. ANOTHER IRAQI WAS KILLED WHILE STANDING ON A STREET CORNER, SERVING AND PROTECTING HIS OWN PEOPLE.

EVERY TIME WE LEFT I HAD 2 MORE RIFLES LOADED AND READY TO GO.

THAT'S NOT COUNTING THE SIDE ARM AND AT-4'S WE CARRIED AROUND WITH US. AT LEAST UNTIL THEY MADE US GET RID OF THEM FROM BEING HUNG ON THE BACK OF TURRETS, WHICH, GIVIN THE SITUATION MAY OR MAY NOT BE A BAD IDEA

AND WHEN YOU SEE A HEAD, DETATCHED YET CARTOONISHLY LIFELIKE, YOUR IMAGINATION CAN GET THE BEST OF YOU. AT LEAST MINE DID TO ME...AND OFTEN...

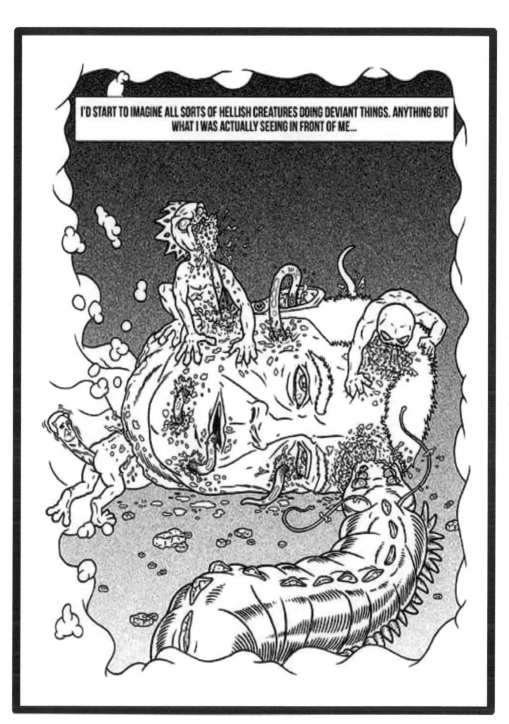

IT TOOK US ALL WINTER TO GET THAT CAR ON THE ROAD BEFORE SPRING AND GOD DAMNIT IF THAT WASN'T A GOOD DAY.

I'M NOT EVEN GOING TO EXPLAIN THE STORY. I JUST HAVE A HARD TIME WRITING ABOUT THIS HORRIBLY DEPRESSING WAR SHIT.

BUT THIS STORY MAKES ME SMILE. JUST SEEING THE IMAGES OF THAT CAR MAKE ME SMILE. MAYBE IT'LL MAKE YOU SMILE TOO.

OKAY, I'LL SAY THIS...

WATCHING THE HOOD OF YOUR '55 CHEVY BEL-AIR FLY OFF WHILE SHIFTING GEARS AT 50 M.P.H WAS PROBABLY ONE OF THE COOLEST THINGS I'VE EVER. I'LL MAKE SURE TO CHECK THE HOOD LATCH FOR RUST ON MY NEXT ONE...

OKAY, I FEEL MUCH BETTER NOW. BACK TO THE SHIT.

CLEARS THROAT LIKE I WAS SAYING... ON THIS PARTICULAR DAY A MAN WITH A GAPING HOLE IN HIS HEAD NEEDED TO BE CLEARED FROM A CITY STREET

HAMMEL, HOUSTON AND A FEW OTHERS WERE ABLE TO SECURE THE BODY TO THE HUMVEE PRETTY WELL.

UNTIL THE HEAD OF THE SOULESS MAN'S STARE STOLE HAMMEL'S HUMANITY. I MEAN I FRICKEN SAW IT. YOU CAN ACTUALLY SEE SOMEONES HUMANITY LEAVE THEIR BODY IF YOU KNOW WHAT YOU'RE LOOKING FOR.

DO I REALLY NEED TO EXPLAIN WHATS HAPPENING HERE?

I..I CAN REMEMBER SO CLEARY. SO CLEARLY SEEING HAMMEL GET OUT OF THE HUMVEE AND GENTLY FIX THE MANS HEAD.

I REMEMBER LAUGHING. IT'S MY SELF-DEFENCE MECHANISM OF CHOICE, APPARENTLY... BUT GOOD LUCK TRYING TO EXPLAIN THAT TO A JUDGE WHILE YOU'RE HIGHLY INTOXICATED DURING COURT.

You are now leaving
the mind of a
21st Century soldier, the last of
many and the first of none.

-Aaron Lee Marshall

2004/07/09

29/09/2004

01/08/2004

20/12/2004

25/12/2004

17/10/2004

2004/07/09

21

All photos courtesy of Tom Jones
(Veteran and the King of Breakfast in

Chapter 13 A Memory?

"You gain strength, courage and confidence by every experience in which you really stop to look fear in the face. You must do the thing you think you cannot do." –Eleanor Roosevelt

I don't remember the specifics about the mission we were on, but the monsters were already with us. We just didn't know it.

We were traveling down route Irish in Baghdad, and the enemy had a different idea about the condition we should be in when we arrived at our destination. I was in the turret of the lead vehicle and Specialist Garneau was in the turret of the vehicle directly behind me. We were heading down what was known at the time as, "The Deadliest Road in the World." I just happened to be looking back at Garneau's vehicle and was just about to take a sip of coke when I saw a huge fireball and explosion completely engulf his vehicle.

I remember holding the can of coke in front of me, the colors of the can popping out at me. There were buildings in the distance and the dark of night was a stark contrast to myself which was illuminated by the lights of the vehicle behind me. Then the Humvee behind us literally disappeared in a ball of fire.

A split second later it came bursting out of the flames still rolling. It was like a scene out of a Quinten Tarantino movie. It was another moment in a long series of events that completely burnt themselves into my brain.

I have forgotten a lot from our tour, but I will never forget moments like that. Lt. Pearson ordered us to stop so we could take care of the vehicle which I'm sure he thought was disabled and then get our guys the hell out of there. But from the turret I could see that the vehicle was still operational, so I let Lt. Pearson know. He then ordered the vehicles to keep rolling through the ambush and on to our destination, which was just about in sight.

Out of all the people in our squad, Garneau was the only one that wore every piece of safety gear. You couldn't see a piece of his skin from behind all the gear he was wearing. I used to make fun of him for wearing all the gear. But it's a good goddamn thing he did because the gear saved his ass from being singed like a chicken kabob at a backyard barbeque. If it had been anyone else, it would have ended very badly. But Garneau wound up being flown out of Baghdad to recover and we all stayed overnight at the airport in a large hanger.

I ended up befriending an American contractor who asked me what had happened. He then said to me, "You look like you could use a drink," and produced a giant bottle of Jack Daniels from under his desk. I said, "Hell yeah, first drink of American Whiskey I've had in months!"

So, he dumped out a soda can and filled it to the brim with Jack Daniels. I then went back to where everyone else was hanging out and told SPC Hatch to take a drink. He had no idea it was whiskey. So, he takes a huge gulp and then his eyes light up and you can literally see the fireball that's about to come out of his mouth. He passed it back and said, "Jesus

Christ Marshall, I thought it was coke," as he laughed and thanked me at the same time. I said, "You're welcome buddy."

The following is a word for word statement by Specialist Garneau via email in December of 2015: The mission was guarding the IP recruits at Warhorse while they waited for their flights to Bagdad international airport. They were being flown to Jordan for training. We left later than we were supposed to be on the road for Bagdad and then Cpt. Pearson got us lost. We were running around the highways down there for almost an hour and a half with at least two stops at Tequila to get directions.

We had just found the right off ramp to the BIAP road at the bottom of the ramp was where the bomb was. This was Chuck Lockhart's first road mission with us, so Sgt Grey was driving.

All I saw was wall of flame coming and closed my eyes and ducked. I was wearing fingerless weightlifter gloves and got first and second degree burns on my fingers and wrists. I was well covered everywhere else, however most of my gear was well cooked. Anything made of nylon got fried, the saw had burn droplet marks on the plastic of the stock and foregrip. The old flack vest on the turret hatch had some holes burned into it. The mirrors on the hummer had the paint burned off them. Kenny just told me to get down after that so they could check me out. I just put my hands in the cooler until we got to the aid station at BIAP. They wrapped my wrists with gauze and sent us onward.

Chapter 14 Fuck You

"Every man is guilty of the good he didn't do." –
Voltaire

In Baqubah some men did more than others. And some men did nothing at all.

One man comes to mind when I think about people doing nothing at all. But you won't see his name mentioned here because trashing a person who let so many people down will do nothing to unite those of us that have been searching for meaning since the War. Dealing with the hell that was Baqubah.

We need to be united in our cause to be there for one another. And even though ten years have passed, and innumerable tragedies have befallen us all, we can start to be there for one another.

And that quote by Voltaire sums it up perfectly. While some men didn't do their duty, in another sense we are all guilty of not doing enough. So why trample on those whose souls will recognize their failings after death? It serves no purpose. The only purpose from what men failed to do, that I see worth any value, is being there for one another, in whatever way fits.

I wasn't a big fan of some of our leadership. By leadership I mean one officer from New Hampshire, and another that wasn't. I'm not using the word leadership as it is defined in the dictionary, because the men I'm talking about showed none of it. I won't mention them by name because I think they are severely misguided human beings not worthy of

150

more than the words I type here. But it's important to note that no matter where you go in life, you're going to run into people like that. And often they are in positions of power. But such is life. Move on. Move forward.

Towards the end of the tour we were on a mounted mission in the south eastern part of Baqubah and we pulled up to an intersection of houses. It was nighttime and the lights shining from one of the houses was completely blinding my line of sight down a road that was in an area I was covering. I yelled to the sergeant to take care of the light, and without hesitation he walked up and smashed the shit out of it with the butt of his rifle like a fucking boss.

Finally, I was impressed.

I've decided to add something that was missing from every earlier version of this book. Just to balance out this chapter. The one soldier that I think we all looked to for reassurance was Specialist Greg Chabot. If I was ever unsure about a situation, which was often, I would look to him. There wasn't one time in 452 days the guy wasn't ready to put a hole in someone or fix a hole in someone, at a moment's notice.

When some Iraqi contractors were hired to change the setup of the rooms, we paid the guy doing the work a literal few dollar bills to leave a few bricks loose in a spot only we knew. Chabot always kept explosives with him and had a sweet draganof rifle that he got from one mission or another. I just liked the fact we could pass grenades in secret. It made me laugh. He was the finest soldier I have ever served with and I depended on him for a lot in Iraq.

Regardless of how our paths diverged once returning stateside, it would be an epic failure on my part to not mention him. He gave up his slot for a 4-day leave to me so I could go to Qatar and get wasted for a few days. He truly was doing what he loved the most and he did not need or want a break from the hell. He deserves to be remembered for the goddamn animal that he was. Not the asshole friend he has become.

I still love you Brother.

Chapter 15 Spoon Man

"When the whole world is silent, even one voice becomes powerful." –Malala

My call sign in Iraq was "Spoon man."

We were told to come up with our own call signs, and I loved the song by Soundgarden, so I went with that. At that point I had never tried heroin and wouldn't until my second divorce about seven years later. But that's a story for another time. An even darker tale of the human experience. Loss. Tragedy. Insanity. And redemption.

Now that I think about it. It was sort of a self-induced experience very similar to Iraq. To War. I relived the terror of death daily with that drug but was one of the lucky few who was able to kick it before it took me completely. I mean that shit took me completely. But I used suboxone for two weeks after my 3 days of the most intense mindfuck I have ever experienced. I've had too many experiences with death. Too many. I swear I'm always looking when some ridiculous shit happens.

I've felt the breeze created by a sniper's bullet gently flow by my face.

I've been hit with anti-tank rockets so close it made me think the world had ended.

I've had septic shock, pancreatitis, renal failure and felt the peaceful calm that comes over you when you die. I even wrote a song about it immediately after. It's called "let those beautiful dreams go" I have no idea where a copy of it is. But it's one of my favorite personal songs. I'm referring to the state of peace I felt as I was being carted into the ambulance as blue as the color of my eyes. My mother had pulled in just as I was being wheeled out and she said she had never seen someone look so blue before. This was before Game of Thrones came out. The first thing I said to her when she told me was, "did you get a picture?" She didn't. Story of my life. Side note I did end up being an Executive Director, in the credits and everything of a film called Deep Clean starring Paul Kaye, who was in Game of Thrones. Even odder his character was a drunken Priest from the Brothers without Banners. Life is weird.

Anyfuckingways.

I've overdosed too many times, and woken up to people standing over me crying...

Yet, I'm still here. I'm still trudging forward. Marching on. To what, I haven't the slightest fucking idea.

I have no idea why I'm still here. Dumb luck maybe? A purpose I don't yet know? I would go with dumb luck over fate. Regardless, I give thanks to the people around me. If I gave thanks to a supposed god, I would be squandering an opportunity to make an actual difference in the world. And I truly fucking believe that.

That was one of the original ideas behind me joining the military in the first place. Trying to make an actual difference in the world.

After September 11th, most young men my age were jolted by a sense of duty to do something. Anything. But still only a few signed up to voluntarily fight in a War that we all knew was coming. We all wanted it. There was that part of the collective unconscious of the country that needed War. Vengeance. Justice.

The same type of situation occurred in Iraq in 2004 when a Sgt. from the 3rd ID and a Lt. ended up both losing one of their arms during an RPG attack on a patrol. We all felt completely helpless immediately after. Here is an account from Sgt. Jim Watson about the event:

On June 19th I was advised that I would be going on a routine patrol mission with the 3rd ID folks at 0300. It was a clear night and the mission was to patrol the local streets of Baqubah. Lt. Halfaker and Sgt. Lara oversaw the mission. I sat behind the driver in the second Humvee in the convoy, while Lara and Halfaker where in the front vehicle in the convoy with Lara in the front seat and Halfaker behind him.

We were not out long before we took small arms fire and I remember we kept looping around to catch the enemy off guard. We crossed a small bride when I saw what appeared to me to be a small flash. The front vehicle paused for a moment and then took off like a bat out of hell. The radio then started going crazy with chatter. I was told to get my aid bag ready as we raced back to the police station. I was not sure why because from my vantage point the Humvee looked fully intact.

We arrived back at the station and luckily there were other medics spending the night with us. I remember radioing ahead to make sure they were downstairs and ready to help. They took Lara out who completed lost his right arm at the shoulder and began to try and stabilize him. I opened the back door and Halfaker was just sitting there in shock. We got her out and laid her on the ground. I remember thinking, 'How the fuck am I going to treat this?'

Her arm was hanging by strands and bone, and blood was everywhere. I just started reacting and doing what I felt might help. I wrapped her arm in gauze and she was given morphine. She kept yelling at me not to put a tourniquet on her. I told her that I was not putting at tourniquet on her but did not have the heart to tell her that her arm was almost gone! I remember everyone watching and encouraging both. We got them into an ambulance, and I thought my job was done.

I was wrong. They told me that I was going to evacuate them to Warhorse as the team lead. I said, 'are you fucking kidding me!?'

The ride seemed very long, and I remember being scared out of my mind that we would be hit again. The window was part way down and I was having a panic attack because it would not go up. I never did get it up.

We arrived safely and unloaded them to awaiting doctors and medics. I then broke down and was crying and hysterical. The medical 1st Sergeant came over and hugged me and told me I did great and probably saved her life. I did not feel that way.

I thought I could have done more and been way more prepared. Morning came fast and we returned to the PD from Warhorse. The mood was sullen, and I was out of it. Not only because I was sad about the two losing limbs, but I realized at that time that I may never make it back to my wife and kids. Everyone was very supportive especially LT Pearson and later Rouleau. The mood stayed this way for several days as I believe we started to realize that this was real!

Searching within ourselves for the answer to the question why? Why did it happen? Why did the RPG enter the front of the Humvee?

like it did? Why that road? Why them? Why not me? And every single man and woman at the Police Station wanted vengeance. Wanted justice.

We knew we would get it, but we just didn't know when. It was part of all our collective unconscious at the station. And we would get it. At least that's how I felt about it.

During one of our QRF missions shortly after the Sgt. and Lt. were severely wounded, we would get our revenge. We needed to kill one of the enemies, a hundred if we could, to make us all feel like we were doing something good for our wounded family. My team got called out to pick up a soldier that had been wounded by an IED just down the road from us on what was called "RPG Alley."

When we went to pick him up, it was a dangerous feeling, a feeling like something bad was going to happen. I'd get that feeling from time to time, and I learned to trust it. Over time that feeling was correct often, and at the very least that feeling would heighten your senses, so you'd be even more ready for an ambush.

You never knew when and if another IED was going to be set off after the first one. But we had to get the wounded out.

The soldier was in good spirits. Pretty bloodied but happy to be getting the hell out of there and onto a base with medical care. Halfway to F.O.B. Warhorse we were ambushed by some AK-47 fire that pinged off the vehicle in front of me then skipped just over our vehicle. I got out of the kill zone by ducking down into the vehicle.

When the gunfire stopped hitting our vehicle my Sgt. yelled, "shoot!" and I popped up, unlatched the turret, swung it counterclockwise, locked the turret back in, and looked down the barrel of my M249 SAW. I didn't even have to aim.

I was looking directly at a man slightly crouched beside a wall, exactly where the gunfire was coming from, holding a weapon. I didn't even think about it. I let loose as many rounds as I could, and I'll never forget how he instantly slumped to the ground when my first bullet hit and stayed motionless as I put about 15 more rounds in him. I ducked back into the Humvee and said the Sgt., "holy shit I got him!" And we called in the confirmed kill.

When I got back to the police station you could see the look of everyone had changed from a somber mood to a look of vindication. None of us ever had a conversation about these feelings. In fact, at least with those I associated with, we didn't really talk about feelings at all. Ever.

The way I perceived it was that we got our revenge for what happened to the Sgt. and Lt. I think that helped us move past the incredible horror of being helpless to them. It helped me move past it, and not dwell on the event so much. Of course, there was nothing we could have done. But you still feel like, and always feel like, there is something you could have done to prevent it.

It's still hard to piece everything together. The entire year. Where to start? How to finish telling it? It doesn't help that I had multiple head traumas while I was there. And multiple head traumas when I returned home. But I'm determined to tell my story. Our story. The story of the 2/197th FA unit that went to Baqubah, Iraq in 2004 as hastily trained MP's.

The Army owned us. And we would all do our part to make sure every one of us got home. We would do our best. And that's exactly what we did. Our best.

I wasn't trained to be a machine gunner in the turret of a Humvee. But by the end of the tour I guarantee I was one of the best. And that's not cockiness in the sense that I thought I was better than anyone else, but a sense of confidence in my abilities. A turret gunner needs that confidence to do his or her job. Without it, fear can creep in and take over, rendering you useless. No, I wasn't better than any other gunner in the War, I was simply one of the best. I hope that makes sense.

To paraphrase one of my favorite schools of Philosophy, the Stoics, and more specifically, Epictetus; there are things in our control like our opinions, desires, and inclinations. There are also things which are not in our control like our body, possessions, honor, and reputation.

So why worry about the things that are not in our control?

Well, that turret and anyone around it that wanted to do us harm was in my control for that year. I made it my mission to be the baddest motherfucker I could possibly be. It was out of my character. But like an actor that gets stuck in role after making a movie, I became a machine gunner. I became the turret. It was my home. That 2-inch-wide strap for a seat was my bed. My home. My church. My religion. And baptism by fire is not an understatement. Some jobs you ask for in the Army, but for the most part you just do what you are told as an enlisted man. And I was told to get in the turret.

I did my job and I did it well.

I still had moments where I slipped though. And later, in the tour I did slip and almost got my buddy Siefken killed.

I didn't almost get him killed, but that's how I thought about it at the time. We were on QRF duty and we had to head out of the compound to hunt down some insurgents. Just as we left the compound and headed south towards Buritz we passed a road where some insurgents were sitting and waiting for us. I didn't see any of them. I must have been looking at the rooftops which is something I did constantly, because this is where they usually were.

But this time, they weren't. I only realized they were there after I heard some machine gun fire and saw some rounds ping off the vehicle behind me where Siefken was in the turret.

Son of a bitch. I fucking missed seeing them. That hadn't happened to me before.

So, we swung back around and went down the road to where the gunfire came from. As soon as we went down that road I opened on a few houses because I was really fucking pissed, I didn't see them the first time around. But they were already gone.

We were also trained to look out for freeway overpasses as possible sites of attack from people throwing grenades and other horse shit. Although in my experience this was complete bullshit.

Chapter 16 One for The Road

"When choosing between two evils, I always like to try the one I've never tried before." –Mae West

We spent a lot of our time just shooting the shit. It was the only real hobby any of us had whether we realized it or not.

We all had different interests, of course. Some people liked to watch DVDs on small portable players or play a game of cards in their spare time. Others liked to read or lift weights.

Something I liked to do when the fighting was at a lull and there wasn't much else to do, was to, "thumb it." I'll have to explain this a little bit. It's a way of masturbating without pulling your dick out of your pants. You just rub the head of your dick in a circular motion with your thumb (hence "thumbing" it) and after a while, and with practice, you're able to make yourself cum.

After months of no female interaction it didn't take that long to get thumbing it down to a science and accomplish the goal after a minute or so. It wasn't just out of boredom because being bored in Baqubah was about as common as random people handing out free one hundred-dollar bills on your local main street. It was about lancing a wound. Draining the devil. Recuperating the realm. Playing ball with god.

Okay, you get the point.

But the real human aspect that kept us all from losing our collective minds was our appetite for conversation. As I listen through the tapes I kept while I was overseas, it becomes apparent right away that humor was one of the biggest tools we used to cope with the disaster around us.

We made fun of everything.

Nothing was out of bounds. At least listening to the tapes that's exactly how it seems.

We made fun of each other, made fun of our wives, made fun of the Iraqis, made fun of everything we loved and everything we hated.

At times when I listen to the tapes it seems like all we did was laugh. But that wasn't the case at all.

Gunshots can be heard in the distance and in one case mortar rounds had just fallen a few feet above me on my bedroom ceiling and put a giant hole in a vehicle just outside my wall... and then we would immediately start joking about the situation.

I remarked in one tape how four to five mortar rounds had just landed and then one hit on the ceiling above our room and we started to move just a bit more quickly after that. And I said it in a joking tone. You can hear the laughter in my voice. It's insane to think about looking back on it.

It was, however, fun as hell, and one of the best ways to keep our minds off the fact we were in one fucked up situation, seeing some extremely fucked up things.

Giving our sergeants shit was one of the most fun activities guys of my rank could do. Especially the ones that were easy to fuck with. That didn't make them bad people or bad soldiers, they did the best they could do, and we were some extremely hard fucking cunts to deal with, but it does make for some fun conversations.

For example; (this conversation is transcribed word for word from one of the many tape recordings I still have from Iraq.)

SGT Smiley: Why you guys standing in the middle? (Talking to SPC Marshall and SPC XYZ.)

SPC Marshall: Why? We are having a quick chat.

SGT Smiley: Listen. If I come over here again, and see you two over here, in the same spot and you're supposed to be over there, and you're supposed to be over there, okay. Fucking, there's going to be hell to pay.

SPC Marshall: (Talking to SGT Smiley) Do me a favor, stand right here, now go stand 15 feet over there and tell me what you see, what's the picture?

SGT Smiley: Look, I don't care, okay. That's a point and that's a point.

SPC Marshall: So, I must literally be standing under the canopy?

SGT Smiley: Don't give me a hard time.

SPC Marshall: I'm not, just asking you a question. Do I have to be sitting or standing under the canopy or is there a specific square I need to be in?

SGT Smiley: Listen here okay, it's not about where you can or can't be okay? You're taking fucking fire, where is your weapon?

SPC Marshall: I have a MK-19 right in front of me.

SGT Smiley: I don't give a fuck about that MK-19!

Long silence takes place and SGT Smiley walks away.

SPC Marshall: (Says to SPC XYZ) He has already been up here twice, he isn't coming up again, he has already missed half of whatever TV show he's watching in the MWR.

This exchange makes me laugh. Mostly because I can picture all the squares on the roof that I'm taking about. They are all a few feet square. But I shouldn't have acted in this way. It was disrespectful to talk to a superior like that and I can promise you I will never do it again.

During one attack against the police station Sgt. Smiliak was wounded by some shrapnel. A piece ripped through one of his testicles and took a piece of one off. Although he claims it grew back. It doesn't matter. The chance for some jokes was already done. When he returned to Baqubah I would randomly start singing a very corresponding line from *Creep* by the Stone Temple Pilots whenever I could.

Look up the line if you don't know the song. It's in the chorus. You'll laugh. I promise.

We also played practical jokes on each other. And I've decided to pepper the stories throughout instead of just having one chapter on military pranks. It breaks up the hell talk of war.

But I got my ass burnt quite a few times. One time that I remember was when I was sleeping peacefully in my bed. God it was nice to finally catch some sleep, which wasn't easy to do in the Baqubah Provincial Police Station. Fucking A! I think I can finally relax!

On this occasion I happened to wake up to a loud explosion that shook the entire building. My first thoughts upon waking were, Jesus fuck, another attack.

So, I immediately got up, grabbed my gear in a cloud of confusion and started heading out to the area where we all met for a briefing before heading out to fight. When I got out there, everyone was just lounging around and looked at me surprised. Like what the fuck are you doing Marshall? I looked back at Siefken and he was laughing his ass off. He was supposed to tell me that we were detonating the explosive pit on the compound. But he decided not to. Nice practical joke huh? I think so. The fucker got me good that's for sure.

Chapter 17 Congratulations!

"Grace arrives, unannounced, in lives that least expect or deserve it... Every day we have smaller, calmer chances to turn another's life around, to serve, to listen. How often do we simply not see what is in front of us? How often do we believe that the world's evils- from terrorism to crime to emotional cruelty- are beyond our capacity to change? Or that there is no one in front of us whom we can serve?" (Andrew Sullivan, essayist and blogger, in When Grace Arrives Unannounced)

I was so sure that I wasn't going to make it out of the war alive that I purposely tried to have a child with my first ex-wife when I was home on my two weeks leave in the early summer of 2004. I would get the news later on in the year that she was in fact pregnant, and a sigh of relief washed over me knowing that my parents would have another child to love, and watch grow if I didn't make it home alive.

It freed up that part of me that was constantly worrying about my loved ones at home. I could fight even harder now, I thought at first, even more care-free. Knowing that I'll live on through my child, whom I may never even get the chance to meet.

I wrote a song called "Gracie's Song," and one of my favorite lines is, "I'm so glad we got the chance to meet." This is because I wasn't sure if I was ever going to be able to meet her, see her, or hold her.

But when I did, I'll never forget thinking the words, "I'm so glad we got the chance to meet."

When I would tell people that I got my wife pregnant and then missed the entire pregnancy, they would say that I planned it out perfectly and was one lucky son of a bitch.

I would joke around and say that I wanted to have a child because I was sure I wasn't going to make it home alive, but that it backfired because I ended up surviving. I know, Har

har. It's just a joke. I love that little girl as much as any father has ever loved a daughter.

Some people assume I'm religious because her name is Grace, and the fact she was also born on Easter morning in 2005. But my ex-wife and I had chosen the name long before she was born.

We both made a list of names and it was the only one that we had in common. I really wanted her name to be Grace Elizabeth Marshall because then her initials would be G.E.M. and she'd be my little "gem" so to speak. I could even put it on a little L.L. Bean backpack. So, after returning home from Iraq I traded my machine guns in for baby bottles and pacifiers. It was one of the best decisions I've ever made.

I was completely certain I was the only person on tour that had a wife that wouldn't cheat on him. Just because of all the other horror stories that I heard from everyone else in Baqubah. I wrote poetry and songs about my ex-wife and caressed my wedding ring daily like a ritual in a religious ceremony. I would take it off and hold it up like Golem and silently say to myself, "My precious", and then laugh to myself, because at the time the *Lord of the Rings* had just come out and my ex-wife and I were huge fans of the movie.

It made me feel closer to home when I did stupid things like that. Even if it was only for a second.

It wasn't easy being a newly married man with a wife who was back home in her senior year of college at a party school. But I had complete faith in her. I even became religious for a time after reading the *Davinci Code*, but I just chalk that up to a 7-day work week and a complete lack of sleep. We did end up getting divorced a short while after I returned home from Iraq, but it wasn't her fault. I was completely distant. I was a different person. And I was trying to hide that fact.

I would pretend everything was alright and tell everyone that I was fine. But that was far from the truth.

The war beat me down and it beat me down hard.

But I didn't have PTSD. Hell no, not me. That was just a myth that was something the weak fuckers had.

The truth of it is, we all have limits. And my seen-too-much-shit-o-meter was overflowing. But while we were there, whether we liked the soldiers we were serving with or not on a personal level, we all wanted to be there for one another. I helped people by covering their ass when I was in the turret. I focused extremely hard on that.

Regardless of how I conducted myself and my distaste for authority without reason, I always put myself out there as a target to cover my brother's asses. I took pride in the fact that others felt safe while I was in the turret behind my M249 SAW. That sweet piece of machine was like my baby.

She held a belt clip of 200 rounds, and you could change to a new one in a few seconds. It is damn awesome.

Chapter 18 Thoughts?

"There was a king in ancient Sumer, who sought eternal life. His name was Gilgamesh. We know of his exploits because the myths and traditions of Mesopotamia, inscribed in cuneiform script upon tablets of baked clay, have survived. Many thousands of these tablets, some dating back to the beginning of the third millennium BC, have been excavated from the sands of modern Iraq."

- Fingerprints of the Gods by Graham Hancock pg. 187

We spent a good amount of time on the road during the tour in Iraq. The threat of an IED was always on our minds, but you couldn't obsess over it too much or it would drive you mad.

Traveling throughout the country was a great way to see some ancient sites. Alexander the Great had conquered these lands and I always thought that was cool. To be fighting on the same patch of land that he and thousands of other Greek and Persian warriors once had. Xenophon also fought his way out of Iraq and back to Greece with the so called Ten Thousand after being abandoned and turned upon.

I would get to cross the Tigris River many times, and still remember a rundown old brick building on the banks of the river called "The Tigris Restaurant." I took a picture of it one day, and I rarely took pictures in Iraq. I could never understand the mentality of people who were always taking pictures of things.

'You're a soldier god damnit!' I would think to myself. 'Not a fucking photographer.' I think it's a bit more important to protect your buddy's ass than to be snapping photos for the kids to view when you get home.

But that restaurant stood out to me in a way. Here was this river I had heard about all my life, and I pictured it in grand ways. It sprang from the belly of the supposed and often named "cradle of civilization," but here was a rundown old brick building, with one table and chair in front, with a guy smoking copious amounts of tobacco in an old wooden chair.

Our ideas about reality change so violently at times that the images become embedded in our brains. Until inevitably, they are changed yet again. And again. And again.

Sometimes it's hard to make sense of it. But I'll never forget that old brick building on the banks of the Tigris, or the old man smoking tobacco in an old wooden chair.

When we got to visit other F.O.B.'s it was amazing to see the comfort that most soldiers lived in. We were all extremely envious of the amount of food choices that were in their mess halls. We were also some of the dirtiest looking soldiers you would run into during the War. Not because we didn't take care of ourselves but because we were constantly working. We didn't get days off. In fact, our "days off" was a day on QRF duty which frequently had us working even harder than on the days we were on patrol or pulling lookout duty.

When I received my ARCOM with Valor which stated:

"PFC Marshall's intrepid actions while under heavy RPG and small arms fire was remarkable. Returning to his fighting position three times after having been thrown clear by the concussion of near direct RPG hits and eliminating the enemy insurgents with his M249SAW and AT4 were truly courageous acts that reflect his warrior ethos. PFC Marshall's dedication

to his fellow soldiers upholds the finest traditions of military service and reflects great credit upon himself, the 3rd brigade combat team, and the United States Army."

I was told by the Colonel who presented it to me that I had the dirtiest Kevlar he had ever seen in the War. I took that as a compliment.

He then told me that what he likes to do, is take his with him in the shower and clean it with soap and water. I thought that was a nice idea. If only I had the time to calmly and quietly clean my helmet in the shower. I just used my knife and occasionally scraped the dirt off. I was too busy trying to keep my fellow soldiers and myself alive to worry about how clean my goddamn Kevlar was.

I remember one mission that took us close to the border of Iran, where we ended up getting a Humvee stuck in the only mud hole for 100 miles. St. Cyr has a picture. We also went to Baghdad a lot and on a few occasions even went to the "Green Zone" there. I always loved the name Green Zone. Like naming an area of land a certain color will make it safe. It was a fuck of a lot safer than every other place we were normally at, but the idea of a "Green Zone" still humored me.

I witnessed more acts of bravery during my time in Iraq than I ever thought possible. Humans are capable of extraordinary things when put to the test.

They are also capable of breaking down. Such is the quality of life, an ever-changing confluence of seemingly random events.

Only after I was stateside for a couple years did I finally come to terms with the reality that PTSD exists. I always thought it was an excuse for people who were too weak to deal with reality. Sure, horrible things happen, but that's part of life, so deal with it and move on.

The problem is our primitive brains don't necessarily work that way. It sounds great in theory, but in action we all cope with trauma in vastly different ways and sometimes we don't even realize that we are doing it.

My brain's way of "dealing" with the trauma was to pretend that it never happened. It was like the memories were scrambled beyond recognition, and if I put too much thought in trying to recall them it became physically painful for me. This wasn't something I was consciously doing. I didn't say to myself, okay, this event was so terrible, I'm just going to forget it ever happened, and let it come back to me in pieces in my dreams. That's a terribly irrational way of dealing with a problem consciously. And unfortunately for me, my choice of dealing with the problems that had built up was to drink them away. And that's one of the worst things you can do, but I didn't realize it for years. Years.

The fact of the matter is everyone deals with trauma in their lives.

Veterans aren't the only people in society that have PTSD. It's a common misconception that only combat veterans can have it. What it really comes down to, is the key factor in any event that can cause it. And that's trauma. Trauma is defined as a deeply distressing or disturbing experience. But I don't think that definition is descriptive enough.

Trauma demoralizes your entire being to the core. It breaks it down so that the fundamental building blocks that have been painstakingly placed there by your psyche become lose and the mind has nothing left to stand on.

It's like being born again but in an even more frightening world and fully aware that the world is a terrible place. And that's all you see. The terrible side of life. The awful things that people do to one another. In that sense it's far from the truth that only veterans can have PTSD. Having PTSD is like living with monsters in your head. Battling it out for the domination of your rational mind.

And it's also a fallacy that you can't recover from a traumatic event.

Unfortunately, in the mind of many people with PTSD, it seems that there will never be an end. It's a case of 'once you know, you can't unknow.'

And this is the exact way in which it seems perfectly reasonable to take your own life. To end the suffering. Even the unknown stretches of death seem preferable to the known events of trauma that have taken place in a person's mind. Especially the unknown. Because maybe there, there is still hope for peace of mind.

This is the way I led myself down the rabbit hole of suicide. And I suspect it's the way many people with PTSD led themselves down as well before taking their own lives. Thankfully I was terrible at trying to kill myself.

When I tried to hang myself, I was so intoxicated I barely remember it. And I certainly don't remember tying the knot, which came undone after what seemed like an eternity and I went toppling to the floor.

The other time something completely unexpected happened.

I was sharing an apartment with a good friend of mine in Franklin, NH, and he wasn't supposed to be home for at least another four-hours. I opened my left arm so gracefully the blood poured out like an Italian fountain. It was beautiful. But just as I was about to sit down in the warm bath I had drawn, there was a loud banging at the door.

My friend got cut early from his job (no pun intended) and didn't have the key and was banging on the door for me to let him in. Shit I thought. This wasn't part of the plan. So, I got out of the tub, wrapped my arm in a towel, threw some clothes on and opened the door. Once he realized what was going on, he said, "Dude, you know there's only one rule of living here. You can't kill yourself."

It made me laugh. To his credit the bastard always knew what to say. It was because of this base honesty I re-evaluated my current situation, bandaged myself up, and abandoned my idea of death. I couldn't do it here. I had promised him I wouldn't kill myself and damnit, the last thing I'm going to do is be called a liar by the one person who has always been there for me besides my Mother, and knows more about my true self than anyone else. I wasn't going to be called a liar in the grave by him.

Sure, I will be called a liar by a lot of people when I die, but not by people I care about. And with that I realized I did still care about things and that thread of humanity helped keep me alive for a long time. It was probably the only thing keeping me alive. Only until I went to rehab and finally got clean and sober did I truly start to appreciate things again. But thank sweet baby Jesus for that friend.

Sometimes all it takes to save a life is honesty from a friend. As Henry Wadsworth Longfellow once said, "And the song, from beginning to end, I found again in the heart of a friend."

Chapter 19 He's Not Wrong

"**I loved** when Bush came out and said, "We are losing the war against drugs." You know what that implies? There's a war being fought, and the people on drugs are winning it." –Bill Hicks

After experiencing combat the first few times, I was sure I didn't have a great chance of making it back home alive.

It's not that I wasn't confident in my abilities as a soldier, or that I wasn't confident in the abilities of those around me; it was the nature of the War we were fighting. Every time we got into a firefight, it started as a goddamn ambush.

I also happened to be a turret gunner which meant I was usually one of the first soldiers to be attacked. It made me think that no matter how good you can be as a turret gunner; it would only be a matter of time before your luck ran out.

I did have luck on my side during a mission to retake a police station in a town just south of us in Buritz, which was a hotbed of insurgent activity during our entire tour. It was a scene of carnage on our way in.

There were cars still smoldering from being blown up, and you could smell the scent of death. The insurgents were still at the police station when we arrived, and some other troops were scattered around the area. It was always hard to tell who a target was and who wasn't at first. When you roll into an area, you don't always know where all the friendly troops are at, and if there are any civilians still lingering about that didn't make it out.

As we came to a stop, I could see a few people with weapons on top of a nearby building and wasn't sure if they were friendly or not. As I turned my gun in their general direction, I could see one of them stand up just a little and give me a wave, at which time I could tell he was a U.S. soldier. So, I turned my attention in the opposite direction and saw another U.S. soldier on top of another building. A few moments later I saw him toss a grenade off the building and I knew the enemy had to be close by. Then some gunfire erupted in front of our vehicle that was directed at some Humvees farther ahead. There was a tank there too and that sucker lit up a building with its gun and man did that make some noise.

We ended up retaking the police station, but it was a chaotic scene.

Information doesn't always trickle down to every soldier at a fast pace and it's hard to make out what exactly is going on, especially when there are so many different things going on at once. You have soldiers on a rooftop to your left, more to your right, and you didn't even know they were there as you rolled in. You must make quick judgments because when we were attacked, it usually came from a rooftop and you couldn't keep your guard down for a second.

You had to constantly be thinking about where an attack might be coming from.

Chapter 20 Super Sad

"We learn from experience. A man never wakes up his second baby just to see it smile." –Grace Williams

The day I returned to my first ex-wife from Iraq, her older sister passed away due to complications during a kidney transplant. Her name was Melissa and she was an incredible spirit. Full of life and love.

This event cemented my belief that there isn't a god. How could someone so innocent and sweet be taken so soon? How could someone that shone such a bright light on the world be brought into the nothingness that is death? I witnessed hundreds of deaths in Iraq and not all were adults.

Child deaths were the greatest tragedy of the War, or any War in my opinion. They are the most innocent of all of us, full of wonder and awe at everything around them. Putting their trust in their parents and loved ones that everything will be alright. But not everything would be alright for a lot of them. A lot of them.

In a song I wrote called, "Iraq War Song," one of the main topics is the death of innocent people during the campaign. It also deals heavily with PTSD and a main catalyst for PTSD, at least in my case, was the death of the innocent, who, had absolutely nothing to do with the War. The chorus goes, "Arms, Legs, Heads, the bodies of babies..." Referring to the VBIED that went off near the intersection in front of the Blue Dome and killed over 72 people and maimed or wounded countless more.

I was standing outside the Baqubah Police Station when it went off. It sounded as if the world had ended. There really is no other way to describe it accurately. I'm sure there are many poets who can brilliantly describe the event had they been there. But this poet, is simply at a loss for words. And I hope I always will be, because that means I am describing it accurately in the first place. Nothingness. On the final pass of this I realized I could describe it like this. I'm standing outside the police station with a group of soldiers, when a sound and feelings instantly makes me feel like I'm about to witness the end of the world. The farthest parts of my perspective turn black and then my vision shuts off like a light switch. *Thunk.* I remember nothing else from that day.

The first room I had at the police station I shared with eight other guys. It was one room with two windows facing the west of Baqubah. But after I traded a DVD player, I had for an acoustic Fender guitar, which I eventually burned at the end of the tour, I ended up sectioning off a third of the room for myself and turned it into a sort of speak easy.

We had a lot of liquor, and after I went on my two weeks leave to the states, we had a lot of pot too. That time in Iraq was one of the funniest in my opinion. Not so much for the guys that didn't partake in the fun...

A few of us would get nice and drunk and sing songs and play guitar. We would also take shots while playing video games and it quickly turned into a bar you would walk into back in the states.

I didn't think about it at the time, but it wasn't fair to the other soldiers who just wanted some peace and quiet after a long day of being shot at. Everyone unwinds differently, and I wasn't as respectful as I should have been to the soldiers who didn't share the same tastes in relaxation that I and a few others did.

Luckily, the soldiers who did have an issue, didn't talk to me about it, and it's probably a good thing they didn't, because I was a mean bastard back then, and while they respected me for how hard I fought, they definitely disliked how I conducted myself at times.

So, they ended up talking to our Squad Leader and I was politely given my own room with the two other soldiers that I partied with. We quickly turned that room into a haven of enlightenment. We strung up Christmas lights and put up posters of Jimi Hendrix and the American Flag and took it easy for the rest of the men who didn't share the same passions. We would have long conversations about absurd topics.

It was a great escape from the reality of what was just outside our walls.

Some of the craziest things that ever happened to me, happened in Iraq. On their own they are completely unbelievable.

I don't think the purpose of me writing any of this down is so I can justify my actions. I think the purpose is for me to get over what I did. I feel bad about a lot of things I did. But I'm also not sure if I would have done anything different...

As we get older, some get wiser, and some become bastardized to their beliefs and are never willing to change.

Life is all about change. Accepting that change. Realizing there isn't anything any of us can do about it. We can't control anything.

The best we can do is to live right, live well, and for a purpose that would make our children proud. And if they grow up to be assholes then oh well, you can at least say you tried.

The Iraqi people had mosques situated throughout the city. They prayed five times a day like clockwork, every day of the week. These prayers were also broadcast throughout the city on loudspeakers that were placed everywhere. And every time one of the prayers started all I could think of was that I was in some bad movie that would never end.

"Alllahhhhh, Alllahhh Ackbahhh" "Allllahhhhh, Alllllahhhhh Ackbah". Which means God is great. That was the main prayer that was shouted in a singing tone throughout the day.

I would have nightmares about this prayer. Nightmares where I was sitting on the roof of the building and all I could hear was that chant. Then insurgents would storm into the compound killing everyone and I was helpless to do anything about it.

These nightmares continue to this day.

When I first returned stateside, they happened every night. So much so I would try to black out from drinking every night so I wouldn't dream at all. But that stopped working after a while.

It's a terrible solution to a real problem. It led to me having terrible insomnia, which is still a problem for me. Now I try to deal with it in a more logical way. By staying busy and trying to understand the root causes of the traumatic events of my past.

A way in which I think we can really start to fix the issue of Veteran Suicide is through education. By using information as tool to better understanding. Specifically, to would be veterans that are going through boot camp.

During Basic Training there is ample time to have recruits sit through classes about PTSD. But when I went through Basic Training there were none. I think this needs to change.

We arm our soldiers with the knowledge it takes to keep them alive during War, so why not arm them with the knowledge that it takes to keep them alive after War?

Hopefully they never even have to go to War, but at least armed with the right knowledge, they will be better prepared for what comes afterwards. I think this idea can even be broadened further to include classes being taught about PTSD in secondary school.

Trauma doesn't only affect the veteran. It effects a multitude of people across the entire population.

We all want to be moved. We all want passion in our lives. But sometimes it's hard to take that first step towards what we truly desire. I used drugs and alcohol to move me for over a decade. But most of the time it moved me in the wrong direction, until it came to a point where I couldn't even have a thought unless I was high or drunk.

When I was at my lowest, I could barely take a shower unless I was wrecked. The touch of the water was uncomfortable. The air outside the shower too cold. What a ridiculous thing. Talk about forgetting what really matters in life and living in a cocoon. Now I look forward to showers. I enjoy them. I stay in the moment and try to feel every bead of hot water drop across my body. It's magical. It's the little things...

We forget this when we are using or drinking. The drugs train our body to only like them and embed in our brains that they are the only things truly worthwhile. And it's all a lie. Drugs lie. Alcohol lies. Marijuana is exempt from lies. That stuff is safer than Aspirin.

I'm not saying that these things are evil or don't have their uses. For example, I was recently in the hospital with pancreatitis and was unsure whether I wanted to take any pain medication. But luckily, I did because it truly created relief. My pain was unbearable, and it was completely acceptable to use that drug in those circumstances.

But when you aren't in pain, and an organ isn't leaking enzymes into your bloodstream and about to explode, it isn't okay to take some pain medication just to "be moved," or to get high. Of course, the brain has a great way of rationalizing this. Well, I may not be in physical pain, but the mental pain of the situation is too much. So, we use. We escape. This only piles problems on top of problems.

Some days it's hard to write. Some days my troubles are so heavy it's hard the press the keys beneath my fingertips. How heavy are the troubles? It depends on the thinking, I guess. I need to change the way I think about things. I think we all need to do this at various times in our lives.

It isn't an easy to task to try and recall events from a decade ago. Luckily, I have recordings and the memories of others to aid me in this endeavor. It also isn't easy to summon up the energy to write when I don't feel like it. But I'm trying to keep moving forward.

Through my writing and rewriting and revising I'm discovering a lot about what I didn't know over the last decade, and what I most certainly didn't know while I served in Iraq.

Politics wasn't something that concerned a lot of us while we were serving. We had the mind that we were too busy doing our job to concern ourselves with larger affairs. We were all too busy trying to keep one another safe to worry about who would be elected to this office or that office.

Sometimes the easy route isn't the way to go.

Let me rephrase that, the easy route is almost always never the way to go.

It takes hard work and dedication to see anything through to its end. Sure, you can get lucky and finish a few things with the help of luck, but an overall sense of duty towards some cause needs to be in your mind. If you don't have a cause in mind when doing a task, it becomes meaningless and less likely that you'll follow through with it.

Chapter 21 Fight Club

"Silence is so accurate." –Mark Rothko

It's true that when a lot of soldiers come back from War they become "adrenaline junkies" so to speak, and I was no exception. I had an extreme amount of road rage and even pulled my Beretta out on a few occasions and pointed it at motorists who had passed me.

One time, I was driving down route 16 with my second ex-wife, and a car sped past me on a straightaway. I got extremely pissed off, pulled up beside them while we were traveling over 80 miles per hour and pointed my 9mm Beretta directly at the driver.

The driver immediately hit the brakes and just stopped in the road. I looked back and the car just stayed there as we drove out of sight. I could have used some anger management classes back then. And luckily, I would take some a few years later. But that was the grip the War still had on me.

Craving that rush of adrenaline was still something I didn't even know about at the time. Adrenaline junky? What's that? Like Patrick Swayze and the rest of his gang in the movie *Point Break*? No, I wasn't like that. Those people robbed banks and were criminals. I had a valid reason to pull my gun out on someone.

What a crock of shit huh? I was being affected by PTSD and I was completely ignoring all the signs. It's important to have a release towards prolonged experiences of intense interaction. If I was educated better about PTSD before I went to War, or even mildly educated on it when I returned, I think would have been better able to handle it when I got home.

It's also true that even while serving in a War some people try to seek that same high during their downtime. I was no different.

One form of this that I experienced was when Siefken and I were playing a video game and we were disagreeing about something. We decided that when the game was over, we would drop the controls and start swinging at each other, and as soon as someone said 'give' we would stop. Well, the game ended, we dropped our controllers and Siefken stood. I didn't. I immediately jacked him like a linebacker into a plastic dresser smashing it and everything else that was in the way. I had him pinned down with one arm across his throat and the other raised in the air. I said to him, "Do you give?"

He gave me a death look of 'no' and spit in my face. I punched him as hard as I could straight in his nose. He then looked up even more pissed off and said "give" as the blood started to pool onto the smashed plastic material below. I let him go and that was the end of it.

The next day Siefken and I went down to the makeshift cafeteria, which consisted of a half-dozen plastic tables and chairs. Everyone was looking at us like 'what the fuck happened?' They had heard we got into a fight but couldn't figure out why we were still hanging out with each other. And we just went about our business like nothing ever happened.

What really caused us to behave in this manner?

I think it had something to do with being adrenaline junkies and not even realizing it. We did however have enough respect for one another to put aside the fact that one of us would be considered the winner, so to speak, but it was more than that. It wasn't just about winning. It was about the rush we got from anticipating the fight that was about to take place, and the rush of action we got from doing it.

Of course, I didn't realize that at the time. I was just focused on kicking the shit out of someone. And before I forget, it's worth mentioning that alcohol loves to instigate fights. It loves it.

In Dover a few years later I would fight for fun almost every time I went out. One night I was out with Spooky Graves doing who knows what and I had to be pulled off a gentleman who wanted to fight for fun at some party we randomly showed up to at 1 a.m.

In another sense, it was the same idea behind us using our air conditioner in Iraq, when it was working, as a fridge for our whiskey. It was probably even one of the ideas behind us drinking. Of course, there is the more obvious reason for that. It was a great escape.

You could take the front panel of the air conditioner off and hide a couple of pints in it and then put the cover back on. The whiskey was always Lebanese and tasted like used motor oil. The only problem with this is that the colder the whiskey, the more we could drink.

The one type of drink that I desperately craved in Iraq was a fresh glass of cold milk. As a teenager I could easily drink a gallon a day. I played sports every day and loved the excitement and competition. I was always on the move. Always doing something, and I drank enough milk to feed a small family.

In Iraq, all we had was this type of milk that could be stored and drank warm. I can't even remember what it was called. But the only way you could drink it, and have it taste like anything close to milk, was by pouring it in a bowl of cocoa puffs and then drinking it after the cereal was gone. It was the worst goddamn chocolate milk I have ever tasted, but it did trick your brain for a second into thinking that you were having milk. And it was far better than drinking the stuff all by itself. However, Darren "Moose," Ripley told me he enjoyed it and I believe him. He's a crazy son of a bitch and from Maine, like myself, so you know you can trust him.

Ice was also something I looked forward too. A cold glass of coke on ice. Goddamn that would be sweet. But that wasn't something that was ever going to happen in Iraq. At least not for us.

We did get to experience some other sweet nuggets of war though. Like mortar attacks. The sound of a mortar coming down towards you is menacing. It wreaks havoc on the mind once you've had the pleasure of experiencing them. They sound like a giant whistle filled with bees crashing down towards you.

A bunch of us were standing outside the police station when we were suddenly hit with mortars. One came so close it was as if it was aimed directly at our ears. Like the gravitational pull of our thoughts was dragging it closer to us. And if the fucker would have gone off, we would have all probably been killed.

But it didn't go off. It just stuck in the ground. Just another day in Baqubah. We all had a good laugh about that one but I'm pretty sure we all secretly shit our pants a little. Situations like this were constantly a reality to us. You never knew when the next mortar attack was going to happen. You might be lucky enough to be inside the compound or not on duty at the time.

But sometimes you weren't as lucky and got to experience the mental hell of not knowing where the goddamn things would land. This psychological hell played a big role in my PTSD, as I'm sure it plays a big role in the thousands of other soldiers who have suffered through the same experience.

But Psychological comforts were present as well. Orion's Belt, that crooked kind of "T" shaped stars in the sky is the same constellation I could see out my window as a child, and there was something extremely comforting about that. As far away as I was from home, I felt at ease every time I looked up and saw it. I could almost picture sitting in my bed on Pine Street in Dixfield Maine. To me it was "that crooked T", and it made me feel the warmth of home like a thick blanket on a cold New England night.

I could see the houses and people that I grew up with. I could see the neighbor's dog. The crazy cat lady's cats. Which would make me think about the time I was hitting rocks with a little wooden bat and accidentally broke one of her living room windows. Whoops. It was a complete accident. I was only trying to see how close I could come to the window. I wasn't trying to hit it.

Something else I brought with me from my upbringing in New England is my theory on conservation of one's energy. It's the same basic idea of what Winston Churchill once offered when he said, "never stand when you can sit, and never sit when you can lay down." This annoyed the hell out of my sergeants but to my credit, I was only late for a shift once by five-minutes during the entire tour.

For 452 days of Active duty, and to quote many people in Maine, "That ain't bad." I liked to stay in bed and sleep for as long as I could. This meant if my shift started at 4:00 o'clock I would be there at 3:59 with 15 seconds to spare.

The Army was getting a hell of a lot out of me. But for the few moments I wasn't holding a machine gun, they were my own. And I would be damned if I would spend any more time than I had to by hurrying up and waiting.

Chapter 22 Is it over?

"Knowing that people can kill is far different from seeing the proof." –Sarah Perry

Towards the end of the tour the action slowed down; always just enough to try and lull you into being unprepared until something inevitably happened again. It was just another bright and sunny day in Baqubah, and I happened to be stationed on OP 1 facing the northeast portion of the city.

Your eyes would always immediately go towards the busy intersection just a few hundred meters away because it was usually sprawling with traffic and every type of uncoordinated idiot you could imagine behind the wheel of a vehicle. Orange and white checkered taxi cabs darted in all directions and just about every other car on the road seemed to be a Toyota.

I would end up buying a Toyota a few years after I came back to the United States for this reason. I saw more Toyotas get blown up and shot to shit in Iraq than any other type of vehicle and often, those fuckers would just keep on trucking. I saw a dump truck get hit with an AT4 and blown to shit. The next day an Iraqi came out, changed the tires, and drove the bitch away. Jesus.

That's the type of vehicle I want to own. They can take anything. If they can handle an AT4 and then just have the tires changed and be driven away, imagine how well the fucker will perform on bumpy New England roads!

Now back to that intersection overlooking OP 1...

I was looking through my binoculars, scanning my sector, trying to see something interesting, when I saw a truck speeding and weaving. Just as I started to focus on the truck and try to make sense of what was going on, the son of a bitch exploded and I sort of fell back and landed on my ass sitting straight up in the plastic chair that was behind me. Holy shit. Just when you thought you had seen it all.

This was an event I literally witnessed every second of, but only certain parts have been seared into my skull. The weaving of the truck and then the explosion. It happened so violently and quick I could barely make sense of it. And if I wasn't there to see the aftermath of the explosion, I would never have believed I saw anything at all.

Luckily it didn't have the same devastating effect as the IED that killed 72 Iraqis near the same location early on in our tour. I think only five people died. All I can picture is a weaving truck that was violently out of control and then disappeared.

This memory comes back to me, first as a film of the truck weaving, and unlike other memories, this one is in the form of a stock movie reel. A wildly swerving truck dodging traffic. And then pictures. Snapshots like Polaroids.

Chapter 23 Qatar and the Tsunami of 2004

"Life is either a great adventure or nothing."

-Helen Keller

Near the end of December in 2004, Siefken and I went on a four day leave in Qatar. I remember watching the events of the Tsunami in late 2004 that happened in Indonesia on the television at a bar on base. I couldn't feel anything for the thousands upon thousands of people I saw on the TV though. I remember watching the death toll rise well over 100,000 at the time and not feeling anything about it.

I felt inhuman. Christ. If I couldn't be moved emotionally by the tragic death of over 230,000 people swallowed up by the ocean, how would I ever be moved by anything ever again?

Would I be emotionless when my children are born?

Would I be the emotionless man in the back of every room that everyone always talks about?

But I tried not to think about it much and instead got hammered as much as I could.

It wasn't a good starting point for how I would come to cope with things in the years to come.

On our second day in Doha, Qatar, I ended up getting a hand job from an Asian woman that was working as a masseuse in one of the shops on base. She couldn't speak a bit of English. But when she was done massaging me, I laid a twenty down on top of the towel, which began pulsing like a steroid user's neck vein atop my erect penis. She looked unfazed and damn happy to see the cash. She gladly took the twenty and jerked me off under the towel.

I'd be lying if I said it took any longer than 15 seconds.

Hell, it could have only been 5 seconds. A cool wind hitting my dick could have sent me off after months of not having a woman's hands on me. And I'm pretty sure she had done that before. Because the money disappeared like the precision of a pit crew worker, along with about 6-months' worth of my bodily fluids.

Right before we went to Qatar, we went on a mission of money. It was a strange one. At Warhorse we waited around for a while until we were told that we were bringing some money to a bank in Baqubah.

I remember seeing those giant sacks of cash. I knew there was cash inside because I checked. And these were giant duffel bags filled to the brim. For a few moments a couple of us joked about stealing some and then living like kings in Iraq for the rest of our lives.

But that would cause way too many problems, and even taking a few handfuls of the cash wasn't something any of us wanted to do. It was still shocking to see such a large amount of cash that we would just hand over to someone. When we got to the bank on the east side of Baqubah, it felt like we were in a scene out of a bank robbery movie except doing everything in reverse.

It felt like we were smuggling money into the bank. And with an amount that large it was a good possibility that someone might decide to take it if they had known anything about it.

Did anyone know what we were doing? Was someone going to try and take it? That's what we were all thinking.

We were on high alert delivering that money. Having what we estimated to be around $3,000,000 in cash would be a nice score for anyone. It was a tense mission. I felt a hell of a lot better when we were rid of the cash and back at the police station...

One issue with recalling events is that a lot of us from Baqubah suffer from advanced CRS. It's called CRAFT and it stands for "Can't Remember A Fucking Thing." I think you can figure out what CRS stands for.

Chapter 24 Paper Bullets of the Brain

"Language is a virus from outer space." –William S. Burroughs

It was the end of January in 2005. The first democratically held elections in Iraq since who knows when we're taking place and guess what? The lucky bastards of the Baqubah police station would be tasked to head out to polling station after polling station for over 24 straight hours to make sure each place had proper security, enough radios, and other equipment necessary to make the elections a success.

Just another great time to be on the front lines of a War. We were ambushed at least four times by machine gun fire and took sniper fire on multiple occasions.

The moment that stands out to me was when I was nearly shot in the head by a sniper.

The air had a coolness about it. It was night and the darkness seemed to swirl about in a cool blue reflecting the breath of the moon. We pulled up to yet another polling site and most of the squad got out to head to where the Iraqis were and do whatever it was, we were there to do.

I was in my normal spot. In the turret. I had been in Iraq for a year now and the constant worry of being killed wasn't as present as it first was. I became distant to the fact I could be killed at any moment. The reality of it was there, but it didn't bother me as much as it first had. The monsters were there. They were always there; I just tried to ignore them. But that was easy because now, I didn't even know they existed.

I was standing in the Humvee with my body exposed out of the top of the turret, leaning back a little and looking at my machine gun when I felt a breeze flow by my face. I also heard a bullet crackling by. It didn't register to me that I had just been the target of an enemy sniper.

Instead, I calmly looked down at Sgt. Evans who was in the back of the Humvee fiddling with a handheld radio and asked him if he had made a gunshot sound. He furrowed his brow, looked up with a puzzled glare and said, "noooo." Then the rest of the squad who had been at the polling station came running past our Humvee and into their own. Someone yelled out, "get down! We're taking sniper fire!"

I sat there for another moment trying to piece it all together. So that's what it was. Hmm. I started to laugh a little bit and then I got down in the Humvee and we took off to yet another polling site. That mission seemed to never end. I felt like I was in limbo in the first circle of Dante's Hell like a virtuous pagan mingling with unbaptized children. I didn't feel tormented, that would come soon enough.

Hopelessness however was never in short supply.

Chapter 25 Do you hear it?

"I have paid all my debts; I have paid all my dues and now nothing remains but the joy of madness." – Oscar "Zeta" Acosta

When I was ten years old someone crept into my mother's apartment in the middle of the night on High Street in Dixfield, Maine. I woke up to my stepsister, Heather Boulanger, screaming and spinning in circles in the small hallway and bathroom adjacent to the bedroom we were in. My mother and other stepsister, Deven, were sleeping on the pullout couch in the living room, which was connected to a tiny kitchen and the front door. The front door was unlocked to let heat in from the downstairs neighbor, so we didn't have to turn ours on.

I never talked to my mom about the details of that night in a thorough way. I don't think the four of us have ever sat down and gone over that traumatic event, which ended when I heard Deven yelling, "Aaron grab the gun!"

I was attempting to pick up the giant 80's stereo and smash it over whoever was attacking my family in the vast darkness of night. But in that moment, I realized I could make it out the front door if I ran.

My next memory I am turning around to see a shadowy figure come barreling out the front door, stop, turn to me, and then run across the street, down the hill and into the night.

The intruder's shoes and a pack of cigarettes were found at the top of the stairs, along with some other items, including a small knife.

After we left Baqubah, we made a few stops at different bases before we flew out of the country. At FOB Anaconda which is in Samarra, Iraq, Siefken and I went to get something to eat at the DFAC. As we walked towards the building the usually crowded area was completely free of soldiers lining up for a meal. We did walk past a bunch of soldiers that gave us uncertain looks but didn't say a word.

We were talking the entire time and had barely noticed what was going on around us. Then I looked up and saw what looked like an astronaut approaching the front of the building, maybe 50-meters away.

We both stopped what we were doing and looked at each other then looked towards the entrance of the building where the man who was dressed in full bomb gear was standing near a package looking curiously at us. Then someone yelled from a distance, "hey! Get out of there!" So, we went back to where we passed the groups of people who were standing around and asked them what was going on.

They said there was a suspicious package that was being treated as a bomb. I said, "that's nice, then why didn't anyone stop us from going over to it?" The guy said, "well, because you guys have MP armbands on, and you were walking like you knew what the hell you were doing."

Oh, okay that makes it cool. I just laughed a little, said Jesus Christ, and we went back to where we came from and ate some delicious MRE's instead.

Chapter 26 The End

"Success is making art with those you love. "–Gavin Rossdale

Holy shit this place is packed.

It doesn't surprise me though. I am at an event put on by Michelle Romano. The CEO of Roman Media has been a friend for over twenty years now. God, I'm old. Not her! I started babysitting her when she was five.

For a moment I have a flash thought of a few years before this, at the Rochester Opera House, where she graciously spoke to the crowd for me, Lucas Cates, and the rest of my friends. But now, now I'm nervous. She's not here to help me, I'm here to help her.

I'm incredibly high on a mix of cocaine and heroin. She doesn't know that but has known of my struggles with drugs and alcohol and always advocated for my sobriety and health. On this occasion I was losing the battle with addiction.

But now I'm trying to figure out what I'm going to play for the next thirty minutes before the premier of the film. I rarely planned a setlist, because depending on what drugs I was on at the time, it may or may not change what songs I wanted to play. Vinny Vella was in the house. That was cool. He gave a great speech at the end of the night. Something about pizza.

What I kept thinking, while I was staring out at a sea of faces, was how it would be nice to do just one more bump before I started playing.

I fumbled to set my guitar on the stand, which I can't find so it drops harder than I would have liked onto the stage. There was a nice patchwork of giant flowing majestic curtains to the right of me, so I ducked back behind the tangled drapes of justice, as discreetly as a man with lights on him in front of 400 people can and railed a geeker.

I spent ten years running from what happened in Iraq.

Ten years that went by like a turtle shot from a giant fucking slingshot. Most days I spend most of the time pondering whether I've spent that time well and what spending your time well even really means.

Spending time with family? Absolutely.

Teaching those around me the little gems about life that I know. I try.

Trying to learn from those around me? Whenever I can.

And trying to decide what to stay away from and who to stay away from. I think the answer ultimately lies within.

Like all things worth any real value, it takes hard work, and you must start with yourself. Who you are as a human being is an ever-changing thing. What you value one day might change the next. But regardless, the core of who you are never changes.

That part of you that made the same silly faces as a child that you make today.

That part of you that some call the soul. Others say genetics.

And still others say it's all just learned behavior. But regardless of what it really is, it's there. And it always will be.

Authors Note

I have some edition of *Bones and Blood* in front of me, a copy of *After the Eclipse* for reference as I finish up this... Jesus Christ. I just did the math! It has now been 15 years since I started this Gonzoesque quest from a single sperm cell or maybe floating gently, softly, inside an egg? Tape recorder securely adhered to a liquid sack? You fucking know it! Where and when does consciousness originate anyway? At what moment does the soul grab hold and begin the ride?

My thoughts are like silly ghosts doing ancient dances in my head. But I'll get this down. Regardless. I don't do drugs anymore. Or drink. Or chug bottles of Nyquil for fun in the desert. But I am on blood pressure medicine and sometimes when I stand up too fast, I get lightheaded and thousands of distant memories come slamming back into my skull. I will not comment on whether I enjoy the sensation or not.

Okay. Back on track. *Baqubah: Bones and Blood* is best described by Matt Harlock. He said earlier that my recollections of my time at war were, "...born of diaries, audio recordings, and his own experiences which truly mine that place that we might call the juxtaposition of the mad and the mundane."

And he was right. I might have told him. I'm not sure.

So, it's nonfiction but it contains dream segments. Or memories. And memories. Or memories. I guess either. Both?

I've always been a fan of the Cheshire Cat. He has just always made sense to me. The only dialogue that I have in the book comes directly from the audio tapes from Baqubah in 2004. The words are transcribed exactly as they appear on the tape. I will make sure an audio of the words gets uploaded to a website in the future. Check my Instagram for that. @Combatdads.

Alright let's end this.

The book! I'm not suicidal!

Sometimes I must state that and then sign stuff. So, I'm just being careful. After all, I have kids now. Well more kids now. Because I wasn't careful. That's why I am now. Not that I didn't want them all! Are you thinking that!? Jesus that's not cool. Not what I meant. That's the problem with the written word – there is just too much goddamn wiggle room.

It's also worth noting that I have, to help me finish this fucker up, two books from Tangerine Press out of Tooting, London. I'm absolutely in love with everything Michael Curran does and I'm hoping he'll eventually read this and come to an agreement with me so we can do a pressing through Tangerine and make some absolutely stunning works of art. Krent Able or Ralph Steadman would be my first choices for creating an original *Baqubah: Bones and Blood* illustration.

I have the *Autobiography of a Brown Buffalo* by Oscar "Zeta" Acosta and William S. Burroughs *Blade Runner: A Movie* because first and foremost they are beautiful and I intend to make my book similar in subtle ways because of how aesthetically pleasing they are to me. I'm a selfish man. Dawkins was right.

The last thing I need to mention is the Tom Petty candle I have burning now. It's made to look like Jesus in flowing robes except it's my man Tom with some shades on looking as tasty as always.

I'm not religious but I'm certain that lighting this sucker is having a positive effect on me as I type the words you are reading. Well the moment you are having not the one I'm having now. Not now for you, but for me, which will be way in the past by the time anyone reads this.

Thanks for reading this. I hope it helps you or someone you love in some way. I hope it has a positive effect. I hope for a lot of things every day. I think that's a key to happiness. Hope and gratitude. Constant gratitude.

I'm thinking about writing a novel based loosely on Blade Runner: A Movie called *The*. If you want to help, hit me up on Insta. I've also added some tasty declassified duty officer logs from the month of April in 2004, have fun reading those.

And just like at the taping of the LIVE album at the Rochester Opera House I must do this.

........End.

Aaron Lee Marshall

December 2019

DUTY OFFICER LOGS

DAILY STAFF JOURNAL OR DUTY OFFICER'S LOG For use of this form, see AR 220-15; the proponent agency is Office of The Deputy Chief of Staff for Operations & Plans				PAGE NO. 1	NO. OF PAGES

ORGANIZATION OR INSTALLATION 2/197 FA (MP)		LOCATION BAQUBAH POLICE STATION, IRAQ	PERIOD COVERED		
			FROM		TO
			HOUR 0000	DATE 3 APR 04	HOUR DATE 3 APR 04

ITEM NO.	TIME IN	TIME OUT	INCIDENTS, MESSAGES, ORDERS, ETC.	ACTION TAKEN	INL
1	0100	0100	LOG OPENED	LOGGED	
2	0133	0134	CENTAUR 3 DROPPED OFF INFORMANT WHO IS UNDER ARREST	SENT FORCE PRO PERS TO SEC PRIS.	
3	0900	0900	EXPLOSION HEARD 1000M NW, SMOKE ALSO SEEN	LOGGED	
4	0905	0905	IED LOCATED AT N GATE OF FOB WARHORSE, GATE CLOSED	LOGGED	
5	0920	0920	IED AT N GATE FOB WARHORSE EXPLODED	LOGGED	
6	0924	0924	QRF SP TO CAMP GABE	LOGGED	
7	1011	1011	VBIED AT N GATE FOB EXPLODED, 3 WIA DAM TO M1114, GATE STILL CLOSED	LOGGED	
8	1328	1328	N GATE FOB WARHORSE NOW OPEN, W GATE NOW CLOSED	LOGGED	
9	1725	1725	WHITE HURST SPOTTED ACROSS STREET FROM OP1	LOGGED	
10	1745	1745	LOGPAC RP	LOGGED	
11	1818	1818	OUTLAW1C RP	LOGGED	
12	1834	1834	2 SINGLE SHOTS HEARD 200M SE OF OP4	LOGGED	
13	1922	1922	GUNSHOTS 50M S OF OP4	JOC NOTIFIED	
14	1947	1947	RED FLARE SEEN 200M SW OF OP2	LOGGED	
15	1948	1948	FLARE SEEN W OF OUR LOCATION	LOGGED	
16	2125	2130	WHT VAN & WHIT/GRY SEDAN PARKED IN NRTH INTERSECTION. 6 PAX WALKING AROUND	IP'S DISPATCHED	
17	2344	2350	BLAST SEEN NORTHEAST OF STATION (CMOC LOC) IED BLAST 2-3 TNT VIC MC 673346	NOTIFIED CENTAUR X	

TYPED NAME AND GRADE OF OFFICER OR OFFICIAL ON DUTY	SIGNATURE	

DA FORM 1594, NOV 62   PREVIOUS EDITION OF THIS FORM IS OBSOLETE.   USAPPC V3.00

DAILY STAFF JOURNAL OR DUTY OFFICER'S LOG
For use of this form, see AR 220-15: the proponent agency
is Office of The Deputy Chief of Staff for Operations & Plans

PAGE NO.	NO. OF PAGES
1	

ORGANIZATION OR INSTALLATION	LOCATION	PERIOD COVERED			
2/197 FA (MP)	BAQUBAH POLICE STATION, IRAQ	FROM		TO	
		HOUR 2400	DATE 4 APR 04	HOUR	DATE 4 APR 04

ITEM NO.	TIME IN	TIME OUT	INCIDENTS, MESSAGES, ORDERS, ETC.	ACTION TAKEN	INL
1	2400	2359	LOG OPENED	LOGGED	
2	0301	0310	EXPLOSION SEEN 500M SOUTHEAST OF STATION VIC MC 673300 APPROX 10 BLOCKS TNT	NTFD BN, DSPTCH IP	
3	0440	0442	EXPLOSION & RED FLARE SEEN WEST OF STATION	DSPTCH IP, BN NTFD	
4	1000	1000	REPORT OF IMMINENT ATTACK ON STATION	LOGGED	
5	1254	1254	PEOPLE SPOTTED CLIMBING TREES NW OF OP3	NOTIFIED JOC, IPS DISPATCHED	
6	1254	1254	QRF SP - MOSQUE/WARHORSE	LOGGED	
7	1415	1415	UPDATE CPA HQ ARIFAN S OF BAGHDAD TAKEN OVER BY 700 PEOPLE(MAHIS ARMY)	LOGGED	
8	1520	1520	PACKAGED SPOTTED 1000M S OF OP2	JOC NOTIFIED	
9	1535	1535	EXPLOSIONS OBSERVED 2000M E OF OP2	JOC NOTIFIED	
10	1614	1614	POSSIBLE PROTEST OF 35-50 PERSONNEL @ MC 7237	LOGGED	
11	2021	2030	BUS DISABLED BUS 200M SE OF STATION	DISPATCHED IP'S	
12	2110	2113	1 TRACER WENT OVER BUILDING E TO W FIRED FLARE	NOTIFIED CENTAUR X	
13	2153	2154	WHITE FLARE SEEN EAST OF STATION APPROX 200M	NOTIFIED CENTAUR X	
14	2210	2215	JOC ADVISED UPGRADING FORCE PROTECTION	GUARD SHIFTS 2X, QRF READIED	
15	2252	2254	GUNSHOTS HEARD EAST OF STATION, CMOC ENGAGING SUSPICIOUS BOX	CMOC REPORTED ENG. OF BOX	
16	2300	2301	WHITE FLARE SEEN EAST OF STATION	NOTIFIED CENTAUR X	
17	2326	2327	JOC NOTIFIED US OF ICDC ROADBLOCK MC 643344	NOTIFIED CENTAUR SHERIF	
18	2350	2352	RED & WHITE STAR CLSTR SEEN NE OF STATION 220M	NOTIFIED CENTAUR X	

TYPED NAME AND GRADE OF OFFICER OR OFFICIAL ON DUTY	SIGNATURE

DA FORM 1594, NOV 62   PREVIOUS EDITION OF THIS FORM IS OBSOLETE.   USAPPC V3.00

DAILY STAFF JOURNAL OR DUTY OFFICER'S LOG

For use of this form, see AR 220-15; the proponent agency
is Office of The Deputy Chief of Staff for Operations & Plans

PAGE NO.	NO. OF PAGES
1	1

ORGANIZATION OR INSTALLATION	LOCATION	PERIOD COVERED			
2/197 FA (MP) CO	BAQUBAH POLICE STATION, IRAQ	FROM		TO	
		HOUR 0000	DATE 05 APR 04	HOUR 2400	DATE 05 APR 04

ITEM NO.	TIME IN	TIME OUT	INCIDENTS, MESSAGES, ORDERS, ETC.	ACTION TAKEN	INL
1	0000	2359	LOG OPENED	LOGGED	
2	0019	0020	SUSPICIOUS FLASHING LIGHT SEEN SOUTH OF STATION APPROX 200M	DISPATCHED IP'S	
3	0042	0043	3 SHOTS HEARD NE OF STATION 400-500M	NOTIFIED CENTAUR X	
4	0339	0339	RADIO CHECK WITH CENTAUR X	COMMS GOOD	
4	0520	0520	RADIO CHECK WITH CENTAUR X	COMMS GOOD	
5	0654	0655	WITNESSED APPROX 50 PERSONNEL WALKING WEST THROUGH INTER. NORTH OF STATION	NOTIFIED CENTAUR X	
6	0709	0717	35 PROTESTERS GATHERING AT VIC MC 675341	DISPATCHED IP'S	
7	0919	0919	ARC WELDER WILL BE GOING HOT WITH SMALL ARMS AT ICDC RANGE AT 0945	LOGGED	
8	0951	0951	TOLD TO REPORT PERSONS WEARING BLACK ROBES, BANDANA AND GREEN BELT TO CENTAUR ASAP	LOGGED	
9	1006	1006	RAMROD-IED AND SMALL ARMS ATTACK ON RPG ALLEY @ VIC MC 66103857	LOGGED	
10	1038	1038	RPG ALLEY NOW AMBER	LOGGED	
11	1056	1056	QRF SP TO CMOC	BN NOTIFIED	
12	1144	1144	POSSIBLE PROTEST/ATTACK ON POLICE STATIONS + CMOC IN BAQUBAH - HEIGHTENED ALERT	LOGGED, SOG NOTIFIED	
13	1155	1155	BOLO WHITE MAZDA SEDAN TAKING PICTURES OF POLICE STATIONS	LOGGED, SOG NOTIFIED	
14	1257	1257	GRAY AUDI SPOTTED HEADING N OF OP2, HAVE PICTURE	JOC NOTIFIED	
15	1534	1534	ALL FOBS ORDERED BACK TO REGULAR FORCE PROTECTIONS	LOGGGED	
16	1550	1550	FOB WARHORSE ATTACKED, 2 ROCKETS IN FOB, 3 OUTSIDE, N AND W GATES CLOSED	LOGGED	
17	1627	1627	30 BUSES LEAVING UNKNOWN LOCATION HEADING TO KIRKUK	LOGGED	
18	1748	1748	GUNFIRE 350M W OF OP3, DARK-COLORED SMOKE	LOGGED	
19	2000	2013	TRACER ROUNDS SEEN SOUTH OF STATION	NOTIFIED CENTAUR X	
20	2330	2335	SUSPICIOUS CAR SEEN SOUTH OF STATION	NO IP'S TO DISPATCH	

TYPED NAME AND GRADE OF OFFICER OR OFFICIAL ON DUTY	SIGNATURE

DA FORM 1594, NOV 62   PREVIOUS EDITION OF THIS FORM IS OBSOLETE.   USAPPC V3.00

ORGANIZATION OR INSTALLATION	LOCATION	PERIOD COVERED			
2/197 FA (MP) CO	BAQUBAH POLICE STATION, IRAQ	FROM		TO	
		HOUR 0000	DATE 06 APR 04	HOUR 2-22	DATE 06 APR 04

ITEM NO.	TIME IN	TIME OUT	INCIDENTS, MESSAGES, ORDERS, ETC.	ACTION TAKEN	INL
1	0000	2359	LOG OPENED	LOGGED	
2	0254	0254	RADIO CHECK WITH CENTAUR X	COMMS GOOD	
3	0637	00641	9 PAX 3 WEARING BLACK ROBES TRAVELLED N ON ROAD TO E OF STATION	NOTIFIED CENTAUR X	
4	0645	0650	20 PAX WEARING BLACK ROBES CAMPED OUT @ VIC MC 668328	NTFD CENTAUR X & JOC	
5	0706	0710	WHITE SMOKE 500M SOUTH EAST STATION	NOTIFIED CENTAUR X	
6	0711	0717	PERSONNEL FROM ITEM 4 MOVING EAST ON FOOT	NOTIFIED CENTAUR X	
7	0720	0728	OH-58D IN AO SEARCHING FOR INDIVIDUAL ON ROOF @ VIC MC 667335	NOTIFIED CENTAUR X	
8	0953	0953	POSSIBLE IED @ MC 62333747	LOGGED	
9	0956	0956	POSSIBLE IED @ MC 695383	LOGGED	
10	1011	1011	GROUP OF 100 PROTESTORS HAS MOVED FROM CMOC TO GOVERNOR'S MANSION	LOGGED	
11	1053	1053	GROUP OF PROTESTORS HAS GROWN IN SIZE AND NOW HEADING E TOWARDS GOV AND CMOC	LOGGED	
12	1111	1111	IED @ MC 62333747 DETONATED BY EOD	LOGGED	
13	1117	1117	BN REQUESTED IPS AT GOV MANSION FOR PROTESTORS	JOC NOTIFIED	
14	1118	1118	TWO UXOS BROUGHT IN	JOC NOTIFIED	
15	1159	1159	SINGLE SHOT HEARD 100M N OF OP1	LOGGED	
16	1225	1225	POSSIBLE IED 679378 MORTOR ROUND W/BLASTING CAP	LOGGED	
17	1329	1329	IED @ MC 695383 CONCLUDED AS FALSE REPORT	LOGGED	
18	1329	1329	IED @ MC 689388 HAS BEEN DETONATED BY EOD	LOGGED	
19	1625	1625	QRF SP TO CAMP GABE	LOGGED	
20	1846	1846	SINGLE SHOT HEARD W OF STATION	LOGGED	
21	1930	1930	BN REPORT ELEC INTEL OF IMMINENT RPG OR VBIED ATTACK ON POLICE STATION IN BAQUBAH,	SOG/OIC NOTIFIED	
22	2021	2021	SINGLE SHOT HEARD S W OF STATION 250M	LOGGED	
23	2022	2022	SINGLE SHOT HEARD S W OF STATION 75M	LOGGED	

TYPED NAME AND GRADE OF OFFICER OR OFFICIAL ON DUTY	SIGNATURE

DAILY STAFF JOURNAL OR DUTY OFFICER'S LOG

For use of this form, see AR 220-15; the proponent agency is Office of The Deputy Chief of Staff for Operations & Plans

PAGE NO.	NO. OF PAGES
2	

ORGANIZATION OR INSTALLATION	LOCATION	PERIOD COVERED			
2/197 FA (MP) CO	BAQUBAH POLICE STATION, IRAQ	FROM		TO	
		HOUR 2023	DATE 06 APR 04	HOUR	DATE 06 APR 04

ITEM NO.	TIME IN	TIME OUT	INCIDENTS, MESSAGES, ORDERS, ETC.	ACTION TAKEN	INL
24	2143	2143	RADIO CHECK WITH THUNDER 01	COMMS GOOD	
25	2154	2157	WHITE FLARE 400M NORTH OF STATION	NOTIFIED CENTAUR X	
26	2235	2237	WHITE FLARE 400M NORTH OF STATION	NOTIFIED CENTAUR X	
27	2238	2239	ONE SHOT FIRED SW OF STATION 500M	LOGGED	
28	2250	2252	BUS TRAVELLED S FROM N AND DISMOUNTED 15 PAX AT ALLEY WAY SE OF OP2	LOGGED	
29	2309	2310	WHITE FLARE FROM CMOC AREA	NOTIFIED CENTAUR X	
30	2330	2332	8 SHOTS FROM AUTOMATIC WPN 500M N OF STATION	NOTIFIED CENTAUR X	
31					

TYPED NAME AND GRADE OF OFFICER OR OFFICIAL ON DUTY	SIGNATURE

DA FORM 1594, NOV 62   PREVIOUS EDITION OF THIS FORM IS OBSOLETE.   USAPPC V3.00

DAILY STAFF JOURNAL OR DUTY OFFICER'S LOG

For use of this form, see AR 220-15; the proponent agency is Office of The Deputy Chief of Staff for Operations & Plans

PAGE NO.	NO. OF PAGES
1	2

ORGANIZATION OR INSTALLATION	LOCATION	PERIOD COVERED			
2/197 FA (MP) CO	BAQUBAH POLICE STATION, IRAQ	FROM		TO	
		HOUR 0000	DATE 07 APR 04	HOUR 1215	DATE 07 APR 04

ITEM NO.	TIME IN	TIME OUT	INCIDENTS, MESSAGES, ORDERS, ETC.	ACTION TAKEN	INL
1	0000	2359	LOG OPENED	LOGGED	
2	0005	0010	TEST FIRE WEAPON SYSTEMS	LOGGED	
3	0012	0013	RED FLARE SEEN NE OF STATION APPR CMOC	NOTIFIED CENTAUR X	
4	0016	0019	2 WHITE FLARES SEEN 250M OUT 1 N AND 1 NE	NOTIFIED CENTAUR X	
5	0100	0105	15-20 FLASHES 1KM-1.5KM WEST OF STATION @ VIC MC 653337	NOTIFIED CENTAUR X & DSPTCHD IP'S	
6	0115	0116	BAQUBAH POLICE HEADQUARTERS UNDER ATTACK BY UNKNOWN NUMBER OF IND.	NOTIFIED CENTAUR X	
7	0118	0122	ATTACK AT LULL, NO CASUALITIES ATTACK CAME FROM NE VIC MC 668338 SM FIRE ONLY	NOTIFIED CENTAUR X	
8	0139	0139	2/197 2ND PLT UP ON PERSONNEL	LOGGED	
9	0140	0140	293 4TH PLT UP ON PERSONNEL	LOGGED	
10	0144	0144	2/197 HQ AND OPS PERSONNEL UP	LOGGED	
11	0140	0154	CMOC AND GOV MANS. REQUEST AK-47 AMMO	ABLE TO SUR. NTFD CENTAUR X	
12	0204	0204	RADIO CHECK WITH THUNDER 01	COMMS GOOD	
13	0205	0205	RADIO CHECK WITH THUNDER 04	COMMS GOOD	
14	0209	0211	UNABLE TO SUPPORT CMOC REQUEST FOR AMMO 130RD AK-47 & 500RD M249 SENT TO BLUE DOME	NOTIFIED CENTAUR X	
15	0314	0312	2 1/2 KIA TRUCK DRIVING NORTH ON RT 2	LOGGED	
16	0602	0610	EXPLOSION HEARD SE OF STATION VIC MC 672336	NTFD CENTAUR X & DSPTCHD IP'S	
17	0826	0826	SMALL ARMS RANGE WILL BE GOING HOT @ 0900	SOG NOTIFIED	
18	0956	0956	PROTEST IN FRONT OF CMOC, HEADING W ON HIGHWAY 5, APPROX 300 PERSONNEL	LOGGED	
19	1001	1001	INTEL FROM BN: MADHI ARMY UPRISING AGAINST AMERICANS TODAY	SOG/OIC NOTIFIED	
20	1014	1014	PROTEST OF 30-40 PEOPLE IN CIV CLOTHES HOLDING FLAG OF SHIITE CLERIC SADR, HDG S ON MARKET ST	LOGGED	
21	1037	1037	300 PERSONNEL HEADING W TOWARDS CMOC	LOGGED	
22	1115	1115	NOW OVER 500 PROTESTORS ON HIGHWAY 5	LOGGED	
23	1215	1215	FIRE MISSION ON GRID MC 602342	LOGGED	

TYPED NAME AND GRADE OF OFFICER OR OFFICIAL ON DUTY	SIGNATURE

DA FORM 1594, NOV 62   PREVIOUS EDITION OF THIS FORM IS OBSOLETE.   USAPPC V3.00

DAILY STAFF JOURNAL OR DUTY OFFICER'S LOG
For use of this form, see AR 220-15: the proponent agency
is Office of The Deputy Chief of Staff for Operations & Plans

						PAGE NO. 2	NO. OF PAGES 2

ORGANIZATION OR INSTALLATION	LOCATION		PERIOD COVERED			
2/197 FA (MP)	BAQUBAH POLICE STATION, IRAQ		FROM		TO	
		HOUR 1216	DATE 07 APR 04	HOUR 2359	DATE 07 APR 04	

ITEM NO.	TIME IN	TIME OUT	INCIDENTS, MESSAGES, ORDERS, ETC.	ACTION TAKEN	INL
24	1345	1345	ARTY COUNTERFIRE	LOGGED/SOG NOTIFIED	
25	2039	2043	RECEIVED INTEL FROM JOC BLUE DOME WILL BE AGRESSED @ 2200	NOTIFIED OIC	
26	2055	2059	FIRED WHITE FLARES NW OF STATION ON INTEL FROM JOC	NOTIFIED CENTAUR X	
27	2055	2057	INTEL FROM CENTAUR X UNKNOWN # OF IND W/ RPG'S @ VIC MC 65903395 (TWIN BRIDGES)	DSPTCHD IP'S	
28	2118	2122	2-3 TRACER RDS UP INTO AIR 1KM W OF STATION	LOGGED	
29	2125	2127	TRACER RDS UP INTO AIR 500-600M S OF STATION	LOGGED	
30	2146	2146	RADIO CHECK WITH W1	COMMS GOOD	
31	2148	2148	RADIO CHECK WITH OUTLAW 1B	COMMS GOOD	
31	2157	2159	INTEL FROM JOC INDICATES MULTIPLE RPG ATTACKS AGAINST INSTALLATIONS IN AREA	NTFD OIC & THUNDER 06	
32	2202	2202	SM FIRE EAST OF STATION 1KM	LOGGED	
33	2213	2213	RADIO CHECK WITH RIDER 6D	COMMS GOOD	
34	2234	2241	WHITE FLARE OVER N INT. FROM WEST	NOTIFIED CENTAUR X	
35	2238	2241	TRACER RDS W TO E 550M SOUTH OF STATION	NOTIFIED CENTAUR X	
36	2307	2314	EXPLOSION HEARD 700M NORTH	NOTIFIED CENTAUR X	
37	2315	2319	REPORT OF 20 IND. ARMED W/ AK-47 & RPG @ VIC MC 673307	NOTIFIED SOG	
38	2358	2358	MULT TRACERS FROM WEST TO EAST 400M SOUTH	LOGGED	

TYPED NAME AND GRADE OF OFFICER OR OFFICIAL ON DUTY	SIGNATURE

DA FORM 1594, NOV 62   PREVIOUS EDITION OF THIS FORM IS OBSOLETE.   USAFPC V3.00

DAILY STAFF JOURNAL OR DUTY OFFICER'S LOG
For use of this form, see AR 220-15; the proponent agency
is Office of The Deputy Chief of Staff for Operations & Plans

PAGE NO.	NO. OF PAGES
108	

ORGANIZATION OR INSTALLATION	LOCATION	PERIOD COVERED			
2/197 FA (MP) CO	BAQUBAH POLICE STATION, IRAQ	FROM		TO	
		HOUR 0000	DATE 08 APR 04	HOUR	DATE 08 APR 04

ITEM NO.	TIME IN	TIME OUT	INCIDENTS, MESSAGES, ORDERS, ETC.	ACTION TAKEN	INL
1	0000	2359	LOG OPENED	LOGGED	
2	0039		BLACK DRESS, TOP AND BOTTOM, WITH GREEN BRAZIARD, BADGES, SASHES, AND/OR YELLOW AND		
			GREEN HEAD AND ARM BANDS. KILL ON SIGHT	NOTIFIED SOG	
3	0042	0045	TRACER FIRE SEEN SOUTH OF STATION 550M	NOTIFIED CENTAUR X	
4	0225	0228	COBRA H REPORTS INDIVIDUAL WALKING TOWARDS STAION FROM SE	NOTIFIED SOG	
5	0323	0325	3-4 RDS AUTO FIRE 400M SW OF STATION	NOTIFIED CENTAUR X	
6	0503	0507	COBRA H REPORTS 4 PERS IN FIELD @ SE CORNER OF INTERSECTION	NOTIFIED JOC, DSPTCHD IP'S	
7	0515	0516	IP'S SET UP CHECK POINT @ N. INTERSECTION	NOTIFIED COBRA H	
8	0537	0537	4 GUNSHOTS 1KM NW OF STATION	LOGGED	
9	0539	0540	AUTOMATIC GUNFIRE 1KM EAST, DIRECT FIRE AGAINST GABE	LOGGED	
10	0559	0600	WHITE STATION WAGON TRAVELLING N WENT E AT INT.	NOTIFIED JOC	
11	0614	0616	WHITE STATION WAGON TRAVELLING S ALONG ROAD E OF STATION	NOTIFIED JOC	
12	0621	0622	GUN FIRE TO EAST OF STATION	NOTIFIED CENTAUR X-Ray	
13	0814	0814	POSSIBLE IED @ MC 674305	LOGGED	
14	0938	0938	UXO @ MC 7033033920	LOGGED	
15	1013	1013	40+ PROTESTORS HEADING E TO W ON HIGHWAY 5	SOG NOTIFIED	
16	1029	1029	CROWD GROWN TO 250 PROTESTORS ON HIGHWAY 5, CURRENTLY HEADING E TOWARDS CMOC	LOGGED	
17	1105	1105	APPROX. 100 PROTESTORS IN FRONT OF BLUE DOME	LOGGED	
18	1114	1114	GUNSHOTS HEARD 300-350M N OF STATION	NOTIFIED CENTAUR X-RAY	
19	1201	1201	MORE GUNSHOTS 300-350M N OF STATION	NOTIFIED CENTAUR X-RAY	
20	1312	1312	POSSIBLE RPG ATTACK @ 1330 AND/OR 2400 ON GOV OFFICE	LOGGED	
21	1312	1312	SUPPOSED RIOT PLANNED FOR 1300 IN MARKET SQUARE	LOGGED	
22	1318	1318	WHITE STATION WAGON PARKED S END OF BARRICADES FOR 5+ MINUTES	JOC NOTIFIED	

TYPED NAME AND GRADE OF OFFICER OR OFFICIAL ON DUTY	SIGNATURE

DA FORM 1594, NOV 62   PREVIOUS EDITION OF THIS FORM IS OBSOLETE.   USAPPC V3.00

DAILY STAFF JOURNAL OR DUTY OFFICER'S LOG									PAGE NO. 3		NO. OF PAGES	

For use of this form, see AR 220-15: the proponent agency is Office of The Deputy Chief of Staff for Operations & Plans

ORGANIZATION OR INSTALLATION	LOCATION	PERIOD COVERED				
2/197 FA (MP)	BAQUBAH POLICE STATION, IRAQ	FROM		TO		
		HOUR 2314	DATE 08 APR 04	HOUR	DATE 08 APR 04	

ITEM NO.	TIME		INCIDENTS, MESSAGES, ORDERS, ETC.	ACTION TAKEN	INL
	IN	OUT			
46	2356	2359	WHITE FLARE 700M NE OF STATION	NOTIFIED CENTAUR X	
47					
	I				

TYPED NAME AND GRADE OF OFFICER OR OFFICIAL ON DUTY	SIGNATURE

DA FORM 1594, NOV 62   PREVIOUS EDITION OF THIS FORM IS OBSOLETE.   USAPPC V3.00

DAILY STAFF JOURNAL OR DUTY OFFICER'S LOG

For use of this form, see AR 220-15; the proponent agency is Office of The Deputy Chief of Staff for Operations & Plans

PAGE NO.	NO. OF PAGES
1	

ORGANIZATION OR INSTALLATION	LOCATION	PERIOD COVERED			
2/197 FA (MP) CO	BAQUBAH POLICE STATION, IRAQ	FROM		TO	
		HOUR 0000	DATE 09 APR 04	HOUR	DATE 09 APR 04

ITEM NO.	TIME IN	TIME OUT	INCIDENTS, MESSAGES, ORDERS, ETC.	ACTION TAKEN	INL
1	0000	2359	LOG OPENED	LOGGED	
2	0002	0002	UKNOWN # IND W/ AK-47 & RPQ VIC MUFARI TRAFFIC CIRCLE	LOGGED	
3	0005	0006	THUNDER PATROL SENT TO MUFARI CIRCLE AGAINST POSSIBLE THREAT	NOTIFIED THUNDER PATROL	
4	0013	0015	EXPLOSIONS NW OF STATION 1-2 KM	NOTIFIED CENTAUR X	
5	0053	0053	THUNDER PATROL RETURNS FROM PATROL	LOGGED	
6	0146	0146	EXPLOSION HEARD 1KM EAST OF STATION	LOGGED	
7	0213	0214	GREEN FLARE DEPLOYED SE IN RESPONSE TO EXPLOSION HEARD 200M EAST OF STATION	NOTIFIED CENTAUR X	
8	0220	0224	STATION RECEIVES SM FIRE FROM VIC MC 669334, ROOF TOP. DEPLOY FLARES, NO MOVEMENT	NOTIFIED CENTAUR X	
9	0230	0230	NO CASUALTIES FROM SMALL ARMS FIRE	NOTIFIED CENTAUR X	
10	0351	0352	RED STAR CLUSTER SW OF STATION 1500M	NOTIFIED CENTAUR X	
11	0405	0406	EXPLOSION HEARD 1500M SW OF STATION	NOTIFIED CENTAUR X	
12	0505	0505	SINGLE SHOT 200M NORTH OF STATION	LOGGED	
13	0521	0522	WHITE FLARE DEPLOYED WEST, TOWARDS BLACK OUT	NOTIFIED CENTAUR X	
14	0530	0538	CALLED IN GREEN & WHITE REPORTS TO CO TOC	2/197 TOC TIKRIT	
15	0908	0908	5.56mm RANGE GOING HOT	SOG NOTIFIED	
16	0943	0943	IED LOCATED @ MC 66413550, IRAQI QRF ON SITE, EOD EN ROUTE	LOGGED	
17	1305	1305	FLYERS FOUND IN STREETS STATING TODAY IS LAST DAY AMERICANS WILL BE IN DIYALA. AN ATTACK IS		
			TO BE EXPECTED AT ANY TIME	LOGGED	
18	1418	1418	WHITE BUS FULL OF PERSONNEL BEEN SITTING 20 MINS ACROSS STREET FROM OP7	JOC NOTIFIED	
19	1421	1421	20 PERSONNEL W/ RPGS LOCATED IN MARKET AREA	LOGGED	
20	1425		AIF ATTACK. STATION RECEIVING SMALL ARMS AND RPG FIRE FROM EVERY DIRECTION. ALL OP'S		
			RETURN FIRE WITH SMALL ARMS, M203, MK19 AND AT-4. FIRE STARTED IN JAIL BY PRISONERS.		
			THUNDER QRF DIRECTED TO SECURE THE PRISONERS AND PUT OUT FIRE. 1 PRISONER KIA, 1 WOUNDED.		

TYPED NAME AND GRADE OF OFFICER OR OFFICIAL ON DUTY	SIGNATURE

DA FORM 1594, NOV 62   PREVIOUS EDITION OF THIS FORM IS OBSOLETE.   USAPPC V3.00

DAILY STAFF JOURNAL OR DUTY OFFICER'S LOG

For use of this form, see AR 220-15; the proponent agency
is Office of The Deputy Chief of Staff for Operations & Plans

ORGANIZATION OR INSTALLATION	LOCATION	PERIOD COVERED			
2/197 FA (MP) CO	BAQUBAH POLICE STATION, IRAQ	FROM		TO	
		HOUR 1425	DATE 09APR04	HOUR 2400	DATE 09APR04

ITEM NO.	TIME IN	TIME OUT	INCIDENTS, MESSAGES, ORDERS, ETC.	ACTION TAKEN	INL
			FIRE UNDER CONTROL. PUNISHER ELEMENT MOVING THROUGH SHIFTA, ENEMY WITHDRAWING.		
			4 CONFIRMED EKIA. 3 US WIA. 2 RETURNED TO DUTY. 1 MEDEVAC TO WARHORSE FOR SMOKE		
			INHALATION. OP'S RESUPPLIED, TROOPS ROTATED, AMMO RESUPPLY FROM FOB GABE.		
21					

TYPED NAME AND GRADE OF OFFICER OR OFFICIAL ON DUTY	SIGNATURE

DA FORM 1594, NOV 62   PREVIOUS EDITION OF THIS FORM IS OBSOLETE.   USAPPC V3.00

DAILY STAFF JOURNAL OR DUTY OFFICER'S LOG For use of this form, see AR 220-15; the proponent agency is Office of The Deputy Chief of Staff for Operations & Plans				**PAGE NO.** 1	**NO. OF PAGES** 3

ORGANIZATION OR INSTALLATION 2/197 FA (MP)	LOCATION BAQUBAH POLICE STATION, IRAQ	PERIOD COVERED			
		FROM		TO	
		HOUR 0000	DATE 10 APR 04	HOUR	DATE 10 APR 04

ITEM NO.	TIME IN	TIME OUT	INCIDENTS, MESSAGES, ORDERS, ETC.	ACTION TAKEN	INL
1	0000	2359	LOG OPENED	LOGGED	
2	0001	0005	CIVILIAN REPORT OF RPG AMBUSH @ MC 674321	NOTIFIED CENTAUR X	
3	0056	0057	SUSPECTED MAHDI HQ @ VIC MC 671346	UPDATED BOARDS	
4	0136	0140	QRF PREP FOR RECON TO W SCHOOL., 3 IND.	NOTIFIED JOC	
5	0141	0144	ODA SPOTTED IND ON SE SCHOOL, WARNING SHOT FIRED	NOTIFIED JOC	
6	0153	0155	QRF SP DIYALA POLICE STATION	NOTIFIED JOC	
7	0244	0244	QRF RP DIYALA POLICE STATION	NOTIFIED THUNDER 6	
8	0258	0300	COBRA 36 HIT WITH 2 RPG @ VIC MC 682335	UPDATED BOARDS	
9	0300	0302	UPGRADE QRF TO REDCON 1	UPGRADED QRF	
10	0416	0416	1 TRACER RD N TO S 800M WESTO OF STATION	LOGGED	
11	0425	0431	RECEIVED MISSION FOR QRF, PATROL S TO MC 667334 TO RD TO E, N BOUND IS ORANGE CIRCL. W BOUND IS		
			TWIN BRIDGES AND E BOUND IS STADIUM. PATROL 0500-0800	NOTIFIED QRF	
12	0459	0500	THUNDER QRF SP FOR PRESENCE PATROL W/ 11 PAX & 3 VEHICLES PATROL 0500-0800	NOTIFIED QRF	
13	0509	0509	COBRA 36 DEPARTS STATION W/ ARC WELDER 6	LOGGED	
14	0649	0651	SENT AMMO, FOOD COUNT TO CENTAUR X : M249 O/H 4,600 REQ 20,000 ; M203 HE O/H 66 REQ 400 ; MK19		
			GREEN ; M16 GREEN ; MRE GREEN ; WATER O/H 500 CASES REQ 1,000 CASES	SENT TO CENTAUR X	
15	0753	0755	POSSIBLE IED VIC MC 668355, IPF ON SITE, IEOD IN ROUTE	UPDATED BOARDS	
16	0753	0755	POSSIBLE IED VIC MC 647401, IP QRF ON SITE	UPDATED BOARDS	
17	0849	0853	INFORMANT SAYS MAJOR ATTACK AGAINST COALITION TARGETS IN AREA TO START 1200	NOTIFIED CENTAUR X	
18	0850	0852	YELLOW PICKUP TRUCK DROVE THRU AREA, SUSPICOUS ACTIVITY.	DISPATCHED IP'S	
19	0916	0919	EXPLOSION HEARD 600M NW OF STATION, SMALL IED	NOTIFIED CENTAUR X	
20	0938	0941	POWER OUT TO STATION	NOTIFIED CENTAUR X	
21	0950	0951	UNKOWN IND IN PALM GROVES TO NW OF STATION	NOTIFIED SOG	

TYPED NAME AND GRADE OF OFFICER OR OFFICIAL ON DUTY	SIGNATURE

DA FORM 1594, NOV 62   PREVIOUS EDITION OF THIS FORM IS OBSOLETE.   USAPPC V3.00

DAILY STAFF JOURNAL OR DUTY OFFICER'S LOG

For use of this form, see AR 220-15: the proponent agency is Office of The Deputy Chief of Staff for Operations & Plans

ORGANIZATION OR INSTALLATION	LOCATION	PERIOD COVERED			
2/197 FA (MP)	BAQUBAH POLICE STATION, IRAQ	FROM		TO	
		HOUR 1116	DATE 10 APR 04	HOUR 2118	DATE 10 APR 04

ITEM NO.	TIME IN	TIME OUT	INCIDENTS, MESSAGES, ORDERS, ETC.	ACTION TAKEN	INL
22	1116	1116	IED @ MC 665340 CLEARED- MK19 RD	LOGGED	
23	1129	1130	IP SUPPORT REQUESTED FOR WEST ALLEYWAY	NOTIFIED JOC	
24	1131	1131	DINA STUDENTS REQUEST IP ASSISTANCE IN EVAC OF UNIV. DUE TO THREATS BY INSURG AGAINST THEM	LOGGED	
25	1133	1133	ARC WELDER 6 INFORMS THAT REQUEST BY DINA STUDENTS COULD BE SETTING AMBUSH	LOGGED	
26	1145	1156	CHANTING AND/OR PROTESTING HEARD TO THE NORTH OF STATION	NOTIFIED CENTAUR X-RAY	
27	1202	1206	BOLO FROM ODA - LIGHT BROWN 11 PAX BUS/VAN W/ BAGHDAD LIC. PLATE #10548	SOG NOTIFIED	
28	1210	1210	VBIED @ MC 677343 - GRAY RENAULT W/ DIYALA LIC. PLATE # 3372	LOGGED	
29	1328	1328	IRAQI SWAT TEAM @ MC 656344	LOGGED	
30	1332	1332	INTEL FROM CHIEF, APPROX 30 GUYS DRIVING NORTH OF BERITZ TOWARDS THIS LOCATION	NOTIFIED CENTAUR X-RAY	
31	1407	1407	INTEL FROM DUKE - 30 PERSONNEL WEARING KHAKI PANTS, YW SHIRTS W/ GREEN SASH OR SHIRT	NOTIFIED SOG	
32	1435	1435	GREEN DOME MOSQUE @ MC 669334 BELIEVED TO BE RALLY POINT FOR ENEMY	LOGGED	
33	1455	1455	GREY AND RED 55PAX BUS W/ BRWN CURTAINS BELIEVED TO HAVE SHUTTLED ENEMY/EQUIPMENT	SOG NOTIFIED	
34	1531	1531	POSSIBLE FIRE MISSION SOON	SOG NOTIFIED	
35	1544	1544	BOLO - 1980 RED TRUCK, POSSIBLY FIRING MOTARS DIRECTED @ CMOC BETWEEN 2000-2200	SOG NOTIFIED	
36	1700	1700	ONGOING FIRE MISSION	SOG NOTIFIED	
37	1804	1804	LOGPAC W/ PRISONERS SP TO FOB WARHORSE	LOGGED	
38	1847	1847	CENTAUR - THUNDER QRF PATROL FOR 10APR04 2300-0200 IN GRAY ZONE	LOGGED	
39	1850	1850	AUTOMATIC GUNFIRE 300-400M W OF STATION	LOGGED	
40	1933	1933	AUTOMATIC GUNFIRE 800M W OF OP4	LOGGED	
41	2054	2054	EXPLOSION EAST OF STATION 100M AWAY	lOGGED	
42	2059	2119	RECEIVED REPORTS OF IPEOD REPORTING TO SCHOOL @ MC 642334, 20 IND W/ AK-47 JUMPED OUT. 9 IND IN		
			GRAY KIA VAN WERE OBSERVING	NOTIFIED SOG	
43	2118	2122	MORTAR IMPACT @ MC 677341 POSS. INJ TO CHILD. IPF RESPONDING TO SCENE	UPDATED BOARDS	

TYPED NAME AND GRADE OF OFFICER OR OFFICIAL ON DUTY	SIGNATURE

DA FORM 1594, NOV 62   PREVIOUS EDITION OF THIS FORM IS OBSOLETE.   USAPPC V3.00

DAILY STAFF JOURNAL OR DUTY OFFICER'S LOG

For use of this form, see AR 220-15; the proponent agency is Office of The Deputy Chief of Staff for Operations & Plans

PAGE NO.	NO. OF PAGES
1	3

ORGANIZATION OR INSTALLATION	LOCATION	PERIOD COVERED			
2/197 FA (MP)	BAQUBAH POLICE STATION, IRAQ	FROM		TO	
		HOUR 0000	DATE 11 APR 04	HOUR 1058	DATE 11 APR 04

ITEM NO.	TIME IN	TIME OUT	INCIDENTS, MESSAGES, ORDERS, ETC.	ACTION TAKEN	INL
1	0000	2359	LOG OPENED	LOGGED	
2	0020	0030	MORTAR FIRE POO VIC MC 672334	UPDATED BOARDS	
3	0021	0030	THUNDER QRF ENGAGING MORTAR POSITION, CURRENT @ MC 675334	NOTIFIED CENTAUR X	
4	0030	0032	THUNDER QRF RETURNS TO STATION FOR REFIT	NOTIFIED CENTAUR X	
5	0040	0046	BULLDOG 16 SP CMOC FOR PATROL TO TAHRIR	NOTIFIED CENTAUR X	
6	0050	0051	BULLDOG 16 IN CONTACT WITH INSURGENT FORCES	NOTIFIED QRF	
7	0058	0100	THUNDER SHERIFF MOVES TO CONTACT IN SUPPORT OF BULLDOG 16	NOTIFIED BULLDOG CENTRAL	
8	0104	0104	CENTAUR SHERIFF CURRENT LOC VIC MC 673334, MAKING TURN FOR CONTACT @VIC MC 682334	LOGGED	
9	0108	0109	BULLDOG 16 SUSTAINS 2 WIA, EVAC'D TO FOR AID STAT. SHRAPNEL NON LIFE THREATENING	NOTIFIED FORWARD AID STATION	
10	0112	0114	SPORADIC GUNFIRE, FIGHT SEEMS TO BE MOVING SOUTHEAST	NOTIFIED CENTAUR 3	
11	0126	0126	2 EXPLOSIONS HEARD SE OF STATION 700M	LOGGED	
12	0132	0132	IP'S REPORT POSSIBLE INSURGENTS AT MOSQUE MC 679328 & @ SCHOOL VIC MC 679327	LOGGED	
13	0130	0137	CENTAUR SHERIFF @ VIC MC 682433000, SUSPICIOUS VEHICLE (POSS VBIED) IN ROAD TO W OF SHERIFF	NOTIFIED CENTAUR 3	
14	0204	0205	SHERIFF ENTERED HOUSE @ VIC MC 683332, WHICH WAS PERCEIVED MORTAR LAUNCH SITE	UPDATED BOARD	
15	0300	0300	TARGET HOUSE CLEARED NEGATIVE RESULTS ON SEARCH. SHERIFF PERFORMING SELF VEHICLE	LOGGED	
16	0314	0314	CENTAUR 3 ASSIGNS THUNDER QRF PATROL SLOT OF 1800 TO 2100 11APR04	LOGGED	
17	0332	0334	AUTOMATIC FIRE SW OF STATION 1KM	NOTIFIED CENTAUR X	
18	0710	0713	LARGE CAL AUTOMATIC FIRE NE OF STATION 200M	NOTIFIED CENTAUR X	
19	0714	0717	AUTOMATIC FIRE NW OF STATION, OTHER SIDE OF PALM GROVE	NOTIFIED CENTAUR X	
20	0930	0930	NUMEROUS EXPLOSIONS HEARD E OF STATION	LOGGED	
21	1001	1001	TEST FIRE 4 240B'S	BN NOTIFIED	
22	1048	1048	FLYERS GOING AROUND TOWN, JOIN FIGHT OR CLOSE SHOPS, REPORT OF 50-100 PERSONS NORTH OLD BAQ.	LOGGED	
23	1058	1058	2 POSSIBLE IEDS, MC 662356, MC 652351 NOT SECURE, POSSIBLE BAIT FOR AMBUSH	LOGGED	

TYPED NAME AND GRADE OF OFFICER OR OFFICIAL ON DUTY	SIGNATURE

DA FORM 1594, NOV 62   PREVIOUS EDITION OF THIS FORM IS OBSOLETE.   USAPPC V3.00

DAILY STAFF JOURNAL OR DUTY OFFICER'S LOG

For use of this form, see AR 220-15: the proponent agency is Office of The Deputy Chief of Staff for Operations & Plans

PAGE NO.	NO. OF PAGES
3	3

ORGANIZATION OR INSTALLATION	LOCATION	PERIOD COVERED			
2/197 FA (MP)	BAQUBAH POLICE STATION, IRAQ	FROM		TO	
		HOUR 2119	DATE 10 APR 04	HOUR 0000	DATE 10 APR 04

ITEM NO.	TIME IN	TIME OUT	INCIDENTS, MESSAGES, ORDERS, ETC.	ACTION TAKEN	INL
44	2123		COBRA H REPORTS WHITE TRUCKS W/RED TARPS, EQ TO 5 TON, APPEARS TO BLOCK HWY 5 BETWEEN		
			CANAL AND CMOC, BULLDOG RESPONDS	NOTIFIED OIC	
45	2130	2136	EXPLOSION EAST OF STATION 100M	NOTIFIED CENTAUR 3	
46	2131	2136	OP1 FIRED FLARE	NOTIFIED CENTAUR 3	
47	2134	2136	SM FIRE EAST OF STATION 300M, NOT DIRECTED @ STATION	NOTIFIED CENTAUR 3	
48	2137	2137	SM FIRE SE OF STATION 100M, NOT DIRECTED @ STATION	LOGGED	
49	2159	2200	TRACER FIRE NE TO SW E OF STATION 100M, COBRA 36	NOTIFIED SOG	
50	2212	2212	COBRA 36 VIC @ MC 686339	LOGGED	
51	2235	2236	TWO EXPLOSIONS HEARD NE OF STATION 600M	NOTIFIED CENTAUR X	
52	2238	2238	COBRA 36 CURRENT LOC VIC MC 661333	LOGGED	
53	2310	2313	JOC REPORTS UNK # IND ARMED W/ AK-47 & RPG	NOTIFIED SOG	
54	2346	2348	2 EXPLOSIONS HEARD 600M NE OF STATION, MORTARS POI 100M N CMOC	NOTIFIED CENTAUR X	
55	2350	2356	DEPLOYING THUNDER QRF TO POO @ VIC MC	DEPLOYED QRF	
56	2356	2357	CMOC ENGAGED SUSPICIOUS VEHICLE VIC @ MC 677338	NOTIFIED SOG	
57	2357	2357	THUNDER QRF SP DIYALA POLICE HQ FOR MORTAR LAUNCH SITE	LOGGED	

TYPED NAME AND GRADE OF OFFICER OR OFFICIAL ON DUTY	SIGNATURE

DA FORM 1594, NOV 62   PREVIOUS EDITION OF THIS FORM IS OBSOLETE.   USAPPC V3.00

DAILY STAFF JOURNAL OR DUTY OFFICER'S LOG
For use of this form, see AR 220-15; the proponent agency
is Office of The Deputy Chief of Staff for Operations & Plans

PAGE NO.	NO. OF PAGES
2	3

ORGANIZATION OR INSTALLATION	LOCATION	PERIOD COVERED			
2/197 FA (MP)	BAQUBAH POLICE STATION, IRAQ	FROM		TO	
		HOUR 1115	DATE 11 APR 04	HOUR 1544	DATE 11 APR 04

ITEM NO.	TIME IN	TIME OUT	INCIDENTS, MESSAGES, ORDERS, ETC.	ACTION TAKEN	INL
24	1115	1115	POSSIBLE STAGING AREA FOR ENEMY VIC MC 675318	LOGGED	
25	1133	1133	INTEL - PROTEST TO BE HELD INFRONT OF BLUE DOME, FOLLOWED BY ATTACK	LOGGED	
26	1210	1210	POSSIBLE IED MC 637347	LOGGED	
27	1230	1230	PRIORITY TARGET WHITE MC 66503375	LOGGED	
28	1300	1300	INTEL - MC 679342 W HYUNDAI SEDAN, SUSPECTED OP	LOGGED	
29	1300	1300	MC 660356 BLUE FORD STN WAGON, SUSPECTED OP	LOGGED	
30	1300	1300	MC 653334 2 SILVER KIA VANS RPG AND PAX	LOGGED	
31	1300	1300	MC 648334 W MITSU. SEDAN, RPGS AND 6 PAX	LOGGED	
32	1315	1315	POSSIBLE IED @ MC 683346, NW OF SOCCER FIELD	LOGGED	
33	1316	1316	HIDESIGHT FOR MORTARS @ MC 686343, WOODS E OF SOCCER STADIUM	LOGGED	
34	1323	1323	1982 WHITE MITSUBISHI 4 DOOR SEDAN, VBIED PACKED WITH TNT	LOGGED	
35	1408	1408	IPS GOING OUT IN CITY IN VEHICLES MARKED WITH DUCT TAPE "X" ON ROOF	LOGGED	
36	1408	1408	IPS ALSO GOING TO CHILDREN'S HOSPITAL @ MC 658343	LOGGED	
37	1410	1410	UNDERCOVER VEC HAVE X ON BACK WINDOW AS WELL AS ROOF	LOGGED	
38	1424	1424	TWO IED ON BOTH SIDE OF ROAD VIC MC652348 MOTORCYCLE SIGHTED NEAR AREA	LOGGED	
39	1432	1432	20 PAX BUS WHITE W/ BLUE STRIP, SAW ENEMY LOAD COFFIN OF WEAPONS NEAR STADIUM AFTER	LOGGED	
			COBRA SWEPT AREA, DISABLE IF SEEN	SOG NOTIFIED	
40	1444	1444	COBRA HOTEL DISABLE WHITE BUS, 3 PAX WEARING BLACK RAN OUT, SECOND BUS FLED NORTH	LOGGED	
41	1446	1446	20 UNARMED PERSONS GATHERING @ MC 640340	LOGGED	
42	1453	1453	W TRUCK SPOTTED HEADING E ON HGHWY 5 TOWARD CMOC, 6PAX W COFFIN IN BACK	LOGGED	
43	1510	1510	R + W BUS HEADING SOUTH, THEN EAST PAST CMOC THEN PROCEDED LEFT 200M DOWN ROAD	LOGGED	
44	1522	1522	GHOST ELEMENT TEST FIRING 240B'S	LOGGED	
45	1544	1544	RANGE GOING HOT	LOGGED	

TYPED NAME AND GRADE OF OFFICER OR OFFICIAL ON DUTY	SIGNATURE

DAILY STAFF JOURNAL OR DUTY OFFICER'S LOG									

DAILY STAFF JOURNAL OR DUTY OFFICER'S LOG

For use of this form, see AR 220-15; the proponent agency is Office of The Deputy Chief of Staff for Operations & Plans

PAGE NO. 3 **NO. OF PAGES** 3

ORGANIZATION OR INSTALLATION: 2/197 FA (MP)

LOCATION: BAQUBAH POLICE STATION, IRAQ

PERIOD COVERED
FROM: HOUR 1834 DATE 11 APR 04
TO: DATE 11 APR 04

ITEM NO.	TIME IN	TIME OUT	INCIDENTS, MESSAGES, ORDERS, ETC.	ACTION TAKEN	INL
46	1834	1834	IEDS ON BOTH SIDE OF ROAD LOCATED @ MC 653351	LOGGED	
47	2032	2032	WHITE FLARE 500M E OF STATION	CENTAUR X-RAY NOTIFIED	
48	2036	2036	ARC WELDER X-RAY REPORTS HELICOPTER COMING IN TO THEIR LZ @ 2130	LOGGED	
49	2042	2042	INTEL - ACCURATE MORTAR AND RPG ATTACK FROM VEHICLES: 2 GRAY OPAL W/ BULLET HOLES IN REAR		
			WINDOW; 1 GOLD LAND CRUISER W/ FLAT WOOD BODY; 1 BLUE KIA; 1 DARK-COLORED DAWOO; ALL		
			VEHICLES HAVE NO PLATES	NOTIFIED SOG	
50	2104	2104	5-7 PERSONNEL W/ RPG/AK47 SEEN HDG N FROM ORANGE CIRCLE VIC MC 666348	NOTIFIED SOG	
51	2156	2158	25 PAX BUS/ IND ARMED W/ RPG'S SEEN IN TAHRIR @ VIC MC 683329	UPDATED BOARD	
52	2208	2208	VERIFICATION OF PRIORTY TGT WHITE, MC 66503375	VERIFIED W/ CENTAUR X	
53	2247	2248	ICE 8 & 9 PROVIDE SECURITY ON TWIN BRIDGES, VIC MC 659339	UPDATED BOARDS	
54	2253	2253	RECEIVED INTEL FROM IP SOURCE THAT ATTACK IS EMMINENT ON STATION	NOTIFIED CENTAUR X	
55	2215	2315	POWER OUT TO AREA WEST OF STATION	NOTIFIED CENTAUR X	
56	2317	2320	CONFIRMED AH-64 SUPPORT FROM CENTAUR 06, ON STATION 0030 HRS, WORKING FOR BN	NOTIFIED CENTAUR SHERIFF	

TYPED NAME AND GRADE OF OFFICER OR OFFICIAL ON DUTY

SIGNATURE

DA FORM 1594, NOV 62   PREVIOUS EDITION OF THIS FORM IS OBSOLETE.   USAPPC V3.00

DAILY STAFF JOURNAL OR DUTY OFFICER'S LOG

For use of this form, see AR 220-15; the proponent agency
is Office of The Deputy Chief of Staff for Operations & Plans

PAGE NO.	NO. OF PAGES
1	3

ORGANIZATION OR INSTALLATION	LOCATION	PERIOD COVERED			
2/197 FA (MP)	BAQUBAH POLICE STATION, IRAQ	FROM		TO	
		HOUR 0000	DATE 12 APR 04	HOUR 1327	DATE 12 APR 04

ITEM NO.	TIME IN	TIME OUT	INCIDENTS, MESSAGES, ORDERS, ETC.	ACTION TAKEN	INL
1	0000	2359	LOG OPENED	LOGGED	
2	0434	0434	RADIO CHECK WITH CENTAUR X	COMMS GOOD	
3	0503	0503	COBRA H REPORTS GUARDS HEAR MORE PRAYER CALLS THAN USUAL TO CENTAUR X	LOGGED	
4	0607	0607	SINGLE GUNSHOT HEARD NE OF STATION 500M	LOGGED	
5	0625	0627	10 IND SITTING IN A CIRCLE, DRESSED IN BLACK S OF STATION ON CANAL ST. NEXT TO TAHRIR APTS.	NOTIFED JOC & CENTAUR X	
6	0710	0715	RECEIVED UPDATED BOLO LIST FROM CENTAUR X, DARK BLUE MITSUBISHI 4DR SEDAN, OLD BLUE		
			MILITARY JEEP, SMALL WHITE STATION WAGON BAGHDAD LIC# 44328, BLUE OPEL OMEGA SEDAN, RED		
			OPEL CAR, GREEN & RED 50 PAX BUS 3 AXLE W/ BROWN CURTAINS, LIGHT BROWN VAN/BUS BAGHDAD		
			LIC # 10548, 1980 TRUCK W/ LARGE BED (POSS. MORTAR LAUNCH SITE)	NOTIFIED SOG	
7	0725	0725	SINGLE SHOT FIRED 250M NE OF STATION	LOGGED	
8	0757	0757	SINGLE SHOT FIRED N OF STATON 100M	LOGGED	
9	0806	0806	TRAFFIC SEEMS A LITTLE LIGHT, BUT SHOPS OPENING	NOTIFIED CENTAUR X	
10	0845	0845	2 SINGLE GUNSHOTS HEARD N OF STATION	LOGGED	
11	0850	0850	COBRA 6 BEGINS SWEEP TOWARDS FOB WARHORSE	LOGGED	
12	0927	0927	IED DETONATED BEHIND COBRA 6, 200M N OF CP 442	LOGGED	
13	0929	0929	PRIMARY AND SECONDARY IED LOCATED @ MC 649349, CORDONING AREA TO ENGAGE W/ 25MM	LOGGED	
14	1014	1014	2 POSSIBLE IEDS @ MC 637348, IRAQI EOD EN ROUTE IN GRAY HYUNDAI	LOGGED	
15	1041	1041	IED LOCATED @ MC 638344, 2 DAISY-CHAINED	LOGGED	
16	1117	1117	MAHDI ARMY SPOTTED BY PRISON COMPLEX @ MC 677348	LOGGED	
17	1122	1122	CENTAUR REQUESTS IRAQI EOD TO START IED SWEEPS, STARTING W/ MC 638344	JOC NOTIFIED	
18	1147	1147	CENTAUR REQUESTS IRAQI EOD TO PICK UP 2 MORTAR ROUNDS DISABLED BY COBRA @ MC 652351	LOGGED	
19	1327	1327	POSSIBLE VBIED HDNG N FROM BAGHDAD, 1992 GRAY AUDI W/ NO LIC. PLATES DRIVEN BY DRIED NOIEL		
			KAMEL; POSS. STOLEN HUMV W/ AUDI MAY HAVE 2 AMERICAN HOSTAGES. ATTACK ON GABE/WARHORSE	SOG NOTIFIED	

TYPED NAME AND GRADE OF OFFICER OR OFFICIAL ON DUTY	SIGNATURE

DA FORM 1594, NOV 62   PREVIOUS EDITION OF THIS FORM IS OBSOLETE.   USAPPC V3.00

DAILY STAFF JOURNAL OR DUTY OFFICER'S LOG

For use of this form, see AR 220-15: the proponent agency is Office of The Deputy Chief of Staff for Operations & Plans

PAGE NO.	NO. OF PAGES
2	3

ORGANIZATION OR INSTALLATION	LOCATION	PERIOD COVERED			
2/197 FA (MP)	BAQUBAH POLICE STATION, IRAQ	FROM		TO	
		HOUR 1328	DATE 12 APR 04	HOUR 2245	DATE 12 APR 04

ITEM NO.	TIME IN	TIME OUT	INCIDENTS, MESSAGES, ORDERS, ETC.	ACTION TAKEN	INL
20	1430	1430	TEST FIRE - M249S	NOTIFIED CENTAUR X	
21	1452	1452	ONCE RCV NEXT REPORT FROM IRAQI EOD ON IEDS, RELAY GRIDS GIVEN TO CENTAUR	LOGGED	
22	1503	1503	LOGPAC SP TO WARHORSE, 7VEC, 24PAX	CPT ADAMS NOTIFIED	
23	1527	1527	5 PERSONS SEEN DIGGING IN GROUND LAYING WIRE S OF SCHOOL THAT IS W OF STATION	JOC NOTIFIED	
24	1602	1602	VBIED UPDATE - GRAY AUDI AND TOYOTA COROLLA SPOT N OF FOB THUNDER BY 82D EN, BELIEVED TO		
			NOW BE IN BAQUBAH	SOG NOTIFIED	
25	1620	1620	COBRA AND IRAQI EOD CLEARED FIRST IED @ 637348, 2 155 UXO'S BROUGHT TO STATION	LOGGED	
26	1630	1630	COBRA AND IRAQI EOD BELIEVE IED @ MC 638344 TO HAVE BEEN MOVED	LOGGED	
27	1705	1705	AUTOMATIC GUNFIRE HEARD 300M W OF OP4	LOGGED	
28	1721	1721	LOGPAC SP WARHORSE 17 VEC,24PAX	LOGGED	
29	1742	1742	LOGPAC RP	LOGGED	
30	1928	1928	THICK BLACK SMOKE SEEN 1000M SE OF OP2	LOGGED	
31	1932	1932	4-5 PERSONNEL W/ RPGS IN SCHOOL TO THE SE, PLAN TO ATTACK TONIGHT OR EARLY TOMORROW	LOGGED	
32	1954	1954	1KM E TO 1KM W OF CEMETARY BRIDGE, VIC MC 665354, 6-8 PERSONNEL SETTING UP POSSIBLE AMBUSH	LOGGED	
33	1955	1955	IEDS LOCATED ALONG HIGHWAY 2, VIC GRID SQUARE MC 6431	LOGGED	
34	2056	2056	SINGLE GUNSHOT HEARD 350M E OF OP2	LOGGED	
35	2057	2057	WHITE FLARE SEEN 500-550M NW OF OP3	LOGGED	
36	2100	2100	WHITE FLARE SEEN 500-550M NW OF STATION	NOTIFIED CENTAUR X	
37	2140	2143	CENTAUR SHERIFF SP'S STATION W/ 14 PAX & 4 VEHICLES FOR CMOC	NOTIFIED CENTAUR X	
38	2151	2152	WHITE STAR CLUSTER X2, E OF STATION 400M	NOTIFIED CENTAUR X	
39	2156	2156	LARGE EXPLOSION NE OF STATION 500M	LOGGED	
40	2225	2225	RED STAR CLUSTER NW OF STATION 1KM	LOGGED	
41	2245	2245	DUKE O REPORTS 25-30 IND W/ RPG, AK-47, PRK @ VIC MC 677347	UPDATED BOARDS	

TYPED NAME AND GRADE OF OFFICER OR OFFICIAL ON DUTY	SIGNATURE

DA FORM 1594, NOV 62   PREVIOUS EDITION OF THIS FORM IS OBSOLETE.   USAPPC V3.00

DAILY STAFF JOURNAL OR DUTY OFFICER'S LOG				PAGE NO. 3	NO. OF PAGES 3

For use of this form, see AR 220-15; the proponent agency is Office of The Deputy Chief of Staff for Operations & Plans

ORGANIZATION OR INSTALLATION 2/197 FA (MP) CO	LOCATION BAQUBAH POLICE STATION, IRAQ	PERIOD COVERED			
		FROM		TO	
		HOUR 2246	DATE 12 APR O4	HOUR 2400	DATE 12 APR 04

ITEM NO.	TIME IN	TIME OUT	INCIDENTS, MESSAGES, ORDERS, ETC.	ACTION TAKEN	INL
42	2254	2254	CENTAUR SHERIFF HAS ESTABLISHED OUTER & INNER CORDON, CONDUCTING SEARCH, NEG CONTACT	LOGGED	
43	2303	2310	25-30 IND MET @ VIC MC 677347, BROKE INTO 5-6 MAN TMS, ARMED W/ RPGS, AK'S MOVING SOUTH	NOTIFIED SOG	
44	2342	2343	COBRA H REPORTS ICDC ENGAGED 2 IND W/ RPG NE OF THEIR POSITION, DPLYNG FLARE	NOTIFIED SOG	

TYPED NAME AND GRADE OF OFFICER OR OFFICIAL ON DUTY	SIGNATURE

DA FORM 1594, NOV 62   PREVIOUS EDITION OF THIS FORM IS OBSOLETE.   USAPPC V3.00

			DAILY STAFF JOURNAL OR DUTY OFFICER'S LOG	PAGE NO.	NO. OF PAGES

DAILY STAFF JOURNAL OR DUTY OFFICER'S LOG
For use of this form, see AR 220-15; the proponent agency is Office of The Deputy Chief of Staff for Operations & Plans

PAGE NO. 1 **NO. OF PAGES**

ORGANIZATION OR INSTALLATION	LOCATION	PERIOD COVERED			
2/197 FA (MP)	BAQUBAH POLICE STATION, IRAQ	FROM		TO	
		HOUR 0000	DATE 13 APR 04	HOUR 2209	DATE 13 APR 04

ITEM NO.	TIME IN	TIME OUT	INCIDENTS, MESSAGES, ORDERS, ETC.	ACTION TAKEN	INL
1	0000	2359	LOG OPENED	LOGGED	
2	0231	0233	WHITE STAR CLUSTER FIRED WEST OF STATION IN RESPONSE TO IP REPORT OF SUSPICIOUS PERSONNEL	NOTIFIED CENTAUR X	
3	0233	0233	SINGLE GUNSHOT HEARD N OF IP GATE	LOGGED	
4	0414	0416	EXPLOSION HEARD SE OF STATION 300M BEHIND OF SCHOOL	NOTIFIED CENTAUR X	
5	0442	0444	GREEN FLARE 175M WEST OF STATION	NOTIFIED CENTAUR X	
6	0530	0541	SAW & HEARD LOUD EXPLOSION UKNOWN DISTANCE, NW OF STATION	NOTIFIED JOC	
7	0859	0859	IED LOCATED @ MC 634354	LOGGED	
8	1006	1006	9MM AND 5.56MM RANGE GOING HOT AT THIS TIME	LOGGED	
9	1042	1042	HOT GATE CLOSED @ GABE, POSSIBLE IED	LOGGED	
10	1130	1130	PLANNED CONTROLLED DETONATION OF IED AT HOT GATE	SOG NOTIFIED	
11	1140	1140	POSSIBLE IED @ MC 642297, UNSECURE AT THIS TIME -- IED AT HOT GATE HAS BEEN CLEARED	LOGGED	
12	1300	1300	EOD DISABLED SECONDARY IED 200M S OF PRIMARY	LOGGED	
13	1303	1303	M249 RANGE GOING HOT AT THIS TIME	SOG NOTIFIED	
14	1341	1341	IED EXPLODED @ MC 642297 EXPLODED WHILE ICDC ON SITE	LOGGED	
15	1423	1423	ELECTRICAL FIRE W OF STATION	LOGGED	
16	1457	1457	MC 662338 POSSIBLE IED BY BLUE DOME, IRAQI EOD AND QRF EN ROUTE	LOGGED	
17	1503	1503	LONG RANGE GOING HOT, 7.62MM	LOGGED	
18	1505	1505	LOGPAC SP, 13PAX, 3VEC	LOGGED	
19	1525	1525	COMSEC CHANGE AT 1545	LOGGED	
20	1847	1847	IED COVERED IN TRASH @ MC 675328 AND POSSIBLE AMBUSH SITE, IRAQI EOD AND QRF EN ROUTE	CLEARED	
21	2021	2021	AUTOMATIC GUNFIRE HEARD NORTH OF STATION	LOGGED	
22	2147	2147	LION ATTACKED @ MC 676387 BY A PLT SIZED ELEMENT FROM N & S SIDE OF RD	NOTIFIED THUNDER QRF	
22	2209	2209	THUNDER QRF SP'S DIYALA POLICE STATION FOR PRESENCE PATROL	LOGGED	

TYPED NAME AND GRADE OF OFFICER OR OFFICIAL ON DUTY	SIGNATURE

DA FORM 1594, NOV 62   PREVIOUS EDITION OF THIS FORM IS OBSOLETE.   USAPPC V3.00

DAILY STAFF JOURNAL OR DUTY OFFICER'S LOG

For use of this form, see AR 220-15; the proponent agency is Office of The Deputy Chief of Staff for Operations & Plans

PAGE NO.	NO. OF PAGES
2	

ORGANIZATION OR INSTALLATION	LOCATION	PERIOD COVERED			
2/197 FA (MP)	BAQUBAH POLICE STATION, IRAQ	FROM		TO	
		HOUR 2210	DATE 13 APR 04	HOUR	DATE 13 APR 04

ITEM NO.	TIME IN	TIME OUT	INCIDENTS, MESSAGES, ORDERS, ETC.	ACTION TAKEN	INL
23	2318	2318	SINGLE TRACER RD SEEN 500M WEST OF STATION	LOGGED	
24	2328	2331	THUNDER QRF REQUEST IP SUPPORT @ MC 668334 FOR VEHICLE AFTER CURFEW	REQUESTED IP THRU JOC	
25	2340	2350	REPORTS SUSPICOUS PERSONS IN WEST GATE ALLEY	REQUESTED IP THRU JOC	

TYPED NAME AND GRADE OF OFFICER OR OFFICIAL ON DUTY	SIGNATURE

ORGANIZATION OR INSTALLATION	LOCATION	PERIOD COVERED			
2/197 FA (MP)	BAQUBAH POLICE STATION, IRAQ	FROM		TO	
		HOUR 0000	DATE 14 APR 04	HOUR 1935	DATE 14 APR 04

ITEM NO.	TIME IN	TIME OUT	INCIDENTS, MESSAGES, ORDERS, ETC.	ACTION TAKEN	INL
1	0000	2359	LOG OPENED	LOGGED	
2	0030	0030	THUNDER QRF RETURNS TO DIYALA POLICE STATION	LOGGED	
3	0458	0459	LARGE EXPLOSION HEARD 1KM SE OF STATION, AFTER EXPLOSION LIGHTS CAME ON E OF STATION	NOTIFIED JOC	
4	0543	0545	AUTOMATIC FIRE 700M NW OF STATION	NOTIFIED JOC	
5	0605	0606	REPORT OF LARGE EXPLOSION 700 M NE OF STATION		
			GHOST 6 REPORTED AN IED DETONATION AT MC		
			676387. SMALL ARMS FIRE REPORTED AFTER		
			DETONATION.	LOGGED	
6	0640	0640	POSSIBLE IED @ VIC MC 648383	UPDATED BOARD	
7	0756	0756	POSSIBLE IED @ MC 677342, IRAQI EOD AND QRF EN ROUTE	LOGGED	
8	0920	0920	IED @ MC 648383 HAS BEEN CLEARED	LOGGED	
9	0951	0951	POSSIBLE IED @ MC 65503385, N OF EASTBOUND LANE ON HWY5	LOGGED	
10	1059	1059	CENTAUR X CALLED TO MAKE SURE OP'S AND GATES ARE PREPARED FOR VBIED ATTACK, NO INTEL JUST		
			WANT TO VERIFY THEY ARE PREPARED	SOG NOTIFIED	
11	1252	1252	SMALL ARMS 500-800M NW OF OP3	LOGGED	
12	1315	1315	SINGLE SHOT HEARD 500-800M NW OF OP3	LOGGED	
13	1322	1322	POSSIBLE IED @ MC 673328, IRAQI EOD EN ROUTE	LOGGED	
14	1421	1421	PRIMARY IED @ MC 655336 DETONATED	LOGGED	
15	1430	1430	DISMOUNTED PATROL CONDUCTED @ MC 652349	LOGGED	
16	1540	1540	COBRA H REPORTED NEW DIRT PILE, N SIDE OF TRAFFIC CIRCLE THAT IS SE OF GOLDEN LADY		
			STATUE, POSSIBLE IED. JOC NOTIFIED AND IRAQI QRF DISPATCHED	JOC NOTIFIED	
17	1851	1851	PROTEST @ MC 668345, SOME INDIVIDUALS MAY BE ARMED	LOGGED	
18	1935	1935	RED PICKUP?		

TYPED NAME AND GRADE OF OFFICER OR OFFICIAL ON DUTY	SIGNATURE

ORGANIZATION OR INSTALLATION 2/197 FA (MP)	LOCATION BAQUBAH POLICE STATION, IRAQ	PERIOD COVERED			
		FROM		TO	
		HOUR 1936	DATE 14 APR 04	HOUR 2400	DATE 14 APR 04

ITEM NO.	TIME		INCIDENTS, MESSAGES, ORDERS, ETC.	ACTION TAKEN	INL
	IN	OUT			
19	1941	1941	REPORT OF 20 VEC AT CEMETARY AND A BROKEN CAR ON W SIDE OF TWIN BRIDGES	LOGGED	
20	2118	2118	SINGLE SHOT HEARD WEST OF STATION 400M	LOGGED	
21	2138	2138	SINGLE TRACER RD N OF STATION 300M, NE DIRECT. OF FLIGHT	LOGGED	
22	2206	2206	GUNSHOTS HEARD 800M NW OF STATION	LOGGED	

TYPED NAME AND GRADE OF OFFICER OR OFFICIAL ON DUTY	SIGNATURE

DAILY STAFF JOURNAL OR DUTY OFFICER'S LOG

For use of this form, see AR 220-15: the proponent agency
is Office of The Deputy Chief of Staff for Operations & Plans

PAGE NO.	NO. OF PAGES
1	

ORGANIZATION OR INSTALLATION	LOCATION	PERIOD COVERED			
2/197 FA (MP)	BAQUBAH POLICE STATION, IRAQ	FROM		TO	
		HOUR 0000	DATE 15 APR 04	HOUR 2400	DATE 15 APR 04

ITEM NO.	TIME IN	TIME OUT	INCIDENTS, MESSAGES, ORDERS, ETC.	ACTION TAKEN	INL
1	0000	2359	LOG OPENED	LOGGED	
2	0206	0215	COBRA H REPORTS 1 VEHICLE W/ 3 DISMOUNTS @ VIC MC 670340	DISPATCHED IP'S THROUGH JOC	
3	0309	0312	EXPLOSION HEARD SOUTH OF STATION 700M	NOTIFIED JOC & CENTAUR X	
4	0328	0335	POWER LOST TO STATION AND AREA S , W, & E OF STATION	NOTIFIED JOC & CENTAUR X	
5	0444	0446	VISIUAL AND AUDIO SIGNATURES ON 3 EXPLOSIONS 1KM WEST OF STATION	NOTIFIED CENTAUR X	
6	0451	0651	COBRA H REPORTED VISUAL @ VIC MC 658343	UPDATED BOARD	
7	0856	0856	LARGE EXPLOSION HEARD MC 706386, WAS A VBIED HITTING A CONVOY ON RPG ALLEY	LOGGED	
8	1040	1042	2 155MM ROUNDS BEING DETONATED @ MC 697203	SOG NOTIFIED	
9	1115	1115	THUNDER QRF SP PATROL OF TAHRIR AND NEW BAQUBAH	LOGGED	
10	1212	1212	RANGE GOING HOT, 5.56MM AND M203	LOGGED	
11	1419	1420	LOGPAC SP	CENTAUR NOTIFIED	
12	1936	1936	OP7 HEARD BURSTS OF AUTOMATIC GUNFIRE BY BLUE DOME	LOGGED	
13	2049	2049	FIVE INDIVIDUALS SEEN IN BUILDING ACROSS ST E OF STATION	LOGGED	
14	2114	2115	TRACER RDS SEEN E OF STATION 400M GOING SW	LOGGED	

TYPED NAME AND GRADE OF OFFICER OR OFFICIAL ON DUTY	SIGNATURE

DA FORM 1594, NOV 62   PREVIOUS EDITION OF THIS FORM IS OBSOLETE.   USAPPC V3.00

DAILY STAFF JOURNAL OR DUTY OFFICER'S LOG

For use of this form, see AR 220-15; the proponent agency is Office of The Deputy Chief of Staff for Operations & Plans

PAGE NO.	NO. OF PAGES
1	

ORGANIZATION OR INSTALLATION	LOCATION	PERIOD COVERED			
2/197 FA (MP)	BAQUBAH POLICE STATION, IRAQ	FROM		TO	
		HOUR 0000	DATE 16 APR 04	HOUR	DATE 16 APR 04

ITEM NO.	TIME IN	TIME OUT	INCIDENTS, MESSAGES, ORDERS, ETC.	ACTION TAKEN	INL
1	0000	2359	LOG OPENED	LOGGED	
2	0050	0052	SHOTS HEARD WEST OF STATION 400M	NOTIFIED CENTAUR X	
3	0317	0317	EXPLOSION SE OF STATION 1KM	LOGGED	
4	0317	0317	LIGHTS OUT ON S & N SIDES OF STATION	LOGGED	
5	0536	0536	AUTOMATIC GUNFIRE 800M WEST OF STATION	LOGGED	
6	0953	0954	US EOD WILL DETONATE AN IED AT OP7 ON FOB GABE IN 10 MINUTES	LOGGED	
7	1018	1018	RANGE GOING HOT, 5.56MM AND 40MM, INDOOR RANGE WITH 9MM	LOGGED	
8	1031	1031	ICDC CHECKPOINT @ MC 692344 ATTACKED BY MORTARS, IRAQI QRF DISPATCHED	LOGGED	
9	1108	1108	US EOD - CONTROLLED DETONATION @ MC 630396	LOGGED	
10	1144	1144	POSSIBLE IED @ MC 691386, IRAQI EOD AND QRF EN ROUTE	LOGGED	
11	1314	1314	RANGE GOING HOT - 5.56MM AND 50 CAL	LOGGED	
12	1418	1418	LOGPAC SP, 3VEC 14 PAX	LOGGED	
13	1451	1451	US EOD WILL DO A CONTROLED DETONATION OF AN IED @ MC 691386	LOGGED	
14	1607	1610	POSSIBLE VBIED,1993 LIMITED ED. BLACK CHEROKEE, TINTED WINDOWS, LARGE DENT IN DRIVER DOOR,		
			CHIPPED PAINT ON THE ROOF, LAST SEEN @ MC 629377 TRAVELING EAST	SOG NOTIFIED	
15	1627	1627	RANGE GOING HOT W/ 5.56MM AND 9MM	LOGGED	
16	1917	1917	EXPLOSION HEARD NW OF OP3	LOGGED	
17	1921	1922	POSSIBLE VBIED SPOTTED IT HEADING S ON CANAL ST, TOOK LEFT BEFORE BRIDGE, HEADED E IN TAHRIR	CENTAUR X NOTIFIED	
18	2304	2304	SINGLE GUNSHOT 200M NW OF STATION	LOGGED	

TYPED NAME AND GRADE OF OFFICER OR OFFICIAL ON DUTY	SIGNATURE

DA FORM 1594, NOV 62   PREVIOUS EDITION OF THIS FORM IS OBSOLETE.   USAPPC V3.00

DAILY STAFF JOURNAL OR DUTY OFFICER'S LOG

For use of this form, see AR 220-15: the proponent agency
is Office of The Deputy Chief of Staff for Operations & Plans

PAGE NO.	NO. OF PAGES
1	

ORGANIZATION OR INSTALLATION	LOCATION	PERIOD COVERED			
2/197 FA (MP)	BAQUBAH POLICE STATION	FROM		TO	
		HOUR 0000	DATE 17 APR 04	HOUR 2400	DATE 17 APR 04

ITEM NO.	TIME IN	TIME OUT	INCIDENTS, MESSAGES, ORDERS, ETC.	ACTION TAKEN	INL
1	0000	2400	LOG OPENED	LOGGED	
2	2027	2030	THUNDER QRF HIT W/ RPG, 1 WIA (SHRAPNEL TO FACE), VIC MC 68213401	NOTIFIED THUNDER 06	
3	2121	2125	SMALL PICKUP TRUCK LEFT @ MC 668340, IPQRF CONDUCTING INVESTIGATION	UPDATED BOARD	
4	2232	2236	WHITE FLARE NW OF STATION 600M	NOTIFIED CENTAUR X	
5	2234	2234	GUNSHOT HEARD W OF STATION 400M	LOGGED	
6	2241	2242	WHITE FLARE NW OF STATION 600M	NOTIFIED CENTAUR X	
7	2253	2253	SEVEN SHOTS HEARD S OF STATION 300M	LOGGED	
8	2323	2323	MULTIPLE GUNSHOTS SOUTH OF STATION 600-800M	LOGGED	

TYPED NAME AND GRADE OF OFFICER OR OFFICIAL ON DUTY	SIGNATURE

DA FORM 1594, NOV 62   PREVIOUS EDITION OF THIS FORM IS OBSOLETE.   USAPPC V3.00

DAILY STAFF JOURNAL OR DUTY OFFICER'S LOG

For use of this form, see AR 220-15; the proponent agency
is Office of The Deputy Chief of Staff for Operations & Plans

PAGE NO.	NO. OF PAGES
1	

ORGANIZATION OR INSTALLATION	LOCATION	PERIOD COVERED			
2/197 FA (MP)	BAQUBAH POLICE STATION, IRAQ	FROM		TO	
		HOUR 0000	DATE 18 APR 04	HOUR	DATE 18 APR 04

ITEM NO.	TIME IN	TIME OUT	INCIDENTS, MESSAGES, ORDERS, ETC.	ACTION TAKEN	INL
1	0000	2400	LOG OPENED	LOGGED	
2	0109	0109	TWO SINGLE SHOTS HEARD N OF STATION 1KM	LOGGED	
3	0917	0917	ARC WELDER RANGE HOT SMALL ARMS SHOTGUN	LOGGED	
4	0918	0923	COBRA HOTEL REQUESTED AN IP PATROL FOR A MAN WHO KNEW OF MORTAR LOCATIONS.	JOC NOTFIED	
5	1655	1655	COMSEC CHANGEOVER AT 1715 KEY 12	COMSEC CHANGED	
6	1657	1710	BOLO 1991 GOLD AUDI BLACK PLATES 12081/ AUTHORIZED TO STOP IT	SOG NOTIFIED	
7	1934	1934	INTEL UPDATE NO IEDS IN AREA, POSSIBLE OP IN TARGET AREA	LOGGED	
8	1954	1954	THUNDER-X QRF REDCON-1	LOGGED	
9	2000	2000	15 TRACER RDS S OF STATION 100M TRAVELLING E	LOGGED	
10	2030	2030	SINGLE TRACER RD 500M SE OF STATION	LOGGED	
11	2051	2053	WHITE FLARE 500-600M SE OF STATION	NOTIFIED CENTAUR X	
12	2100	2109	WHITE FLARE 500-600M SE OF STATION	NOTIFIED CENTAUR X	
13	2100	2109	SMALL ARMS FIRE 400M E OF STATION	NOTIFIED CENTAUR X	
14	2127	2127	SINGLE TRACER RD INTO AIR 2KM N OF STATION	NOTIFIED CENTAUR X	
15	2145	2145	SINGLE SHOT HEARD SW OF STATION 400M	LOGGED	
16	2205	2205	SINGLE SHOT HEARD 800M SE OF STATION	LOGGED	
17	2215	2215	SINGLE GUNSHOT HEARD 500M S OF STATION	LOGGED	

TYPED NAME AND GRADE OF OFFICER OR OFFICIAL ON DUTY	SIGNATURE

DA FORM 1594, NOV 62   PREVIOUS EDITION OF THIS FORM IS OBSOLETE.   USAPPC V3.00

DAILY STAFF JOURNAL OR DUTY OFFICER'S LOG

For use of this form, see AR 220-15: the proponent agency is Office of The Deputy Chief of Staff for Operations & Plans

PAGE NO.	NO. OF PAGES
1	

ORGANIZATION OR INSTALLATION	LOCATION	PERIOD COVERED			
2/197 FA (MP)	BAQUBAH POLICE STATION, IRAQ	FROM		TO	
		HOUR 0000	DATE 18 APR 04	HOUR	DATE 18 APR 04

ITEM NO.	TIME IN	TIME OUT	INCIDENTS, MESSAGES, ORDERS, ETC.	ACTION TAKEN	INL
1	0000	2400	LOG OPENED	LOGGED	
2	0109	0109	TWO SINGLE SHOTS HEARD N OF STATION 1KM	LOGGED	
3	0917	0917	ARC WELDER RANGE HOT SMALL ARMS SHOTGUN	LOGGED	
4	0918	0923	COBRA HOTEL REQUESTED AN IP PATROL FOR A MAN WHO KNEW OF MORTAR LOCATIONS.	JOC NOTFIED	
5	1655	1655	COMSEC CHANGEOVER AT 1715 KEY 12	COMSEC CHANGED	
6	1657	1710	BOLO 1991 GOLD AUDI BLACK PLATES 12081/ AUTHORIZED TO STOP IT	SOG NOTIFIED	
7	1934	1934	INTEL UPDATE NO IEDS IN AREA, POSSIBLE OP IN TARGET AREA	LOGGED	
8	1954	1954	THUNDER-X QRF REDCON-1	LOGGED	
9	2000	2000	15 TRACER RDS S OF STATION 100M TRAVELLING E	LOGGED	
10	2030	2030	SINGLE TRACER RD 500M SE OF STATION	LOGGED	
11	2051	2053	WHITE FLARE 500-600M SE OF STATION	NOTIFIED CENTAUR X	
12	2100	2109	WHITE FLARE 500-600M SE OF STATION	NOTIFIED CENTAUR X	
13	2100	2109	SMALL ARMS FIRE 400M E OF STATION	NOTIFIED CENTAUR X	
14	2127	2127	SINGLE TRACER RD INTO AIR 2KM N OF STATION	NOTIFIED CENTAUR X	
15	2145	2145	SINGLE SHOT HEARD SW OF STATION 400M	LOGGED	
16	2205	2205	SINGLE SHOT HEARD 800M SE OF STATION	LOGGED	
17	2215	2215	SINGLE GUNSHOT HEARD 500M S OF STATION	LOGGED	

TYPED NAME AND GRADE OF OFFICER OR OFFICIAL ON DUTY	SIGNATURE

DA FORM 1594, NOV 62   PREVIOUS EDITION OF THIS FORM IS OBSOLETE.   USAPPC V3.00

DAILY STAFF JOURNAL OR DUTY OFFICER'S LOG

For use of this form, see AR 220-15; the proponent agency
is Office of The Deputy Chief of Staff for Operations & Plans

PAGE NO.	NO. OF PAGES
1	

ORGANIZATION OR INSTALLATION	LOCATION	PERIOD COVERED			
2/197 FA (MP)	BAQUBAH POLICE STATION, IRAQ	FROM		TO	
		HOUR 0000	DATE 19 APR 04	HOUR	DATE 19 APR 04

ITEM NO.	TIME IN	TIME OUT	INCIDENTS, MESSAGES, ORDERS, ETC.	ACTION TAKEN	INL
1	0000	2400	LOG OPENED	LOGGED	
2	0002	0005	EXPLOSION HEARD 1KM S OF STATION	NOTIFIED CENTAUR X	
3	0005	0005	EXPLOSION HEARD 1KM S OF STATION	LOGGED	
4	005	0005	SINGLE GUN SHOT HEARD S OF STATION 700M	LOGGED	
5	0329	0330	POWER IS OFF TO DIYALA POLICE STATION AND SURROUNDING AREA	NOTIFIED CENTAUR X	
6	0813	0814	POSSIBLE IED @ MC 697401, DESCRIBED AS A BOX ALONGSIDE ROAD, IRAQI QRF AND EOD EN ROUTE	LOGGED	
7	0919	0919	CLEAN-UP CREW WILL BE IN AO FOR REMAINDER OF WEEK, WEARING ORANGE REFLECTOR VESTS AND		
			CARRYING SHOVELS, NO DETAINING OR QUESTIONING THEM	LOGGED	
8	1812	1812	GUNFIRE HEARD 300M SE OF STATION, BELIEVED TO BE WEDDING	LOGGED	
9	1910	1910	GUNSHOTS HEARD 300M SE OF STATION	LOGGED	
10	1919	1919	MULTIPLE GUNSHOTS HEARD 200M E OF STATION	LOGGED	
11	2234	2236	QRF SENT OUT TO VIC MC 644344 IN SUPPORT TO INSURGENT ACTIVITY	QRF SENT	
12	2259	2259	TWO GUNSHOTS HEARD 300M SOUTH	LOGGED	
13	2309	2309	SINGLE TRACER RD 400M W OF STATION TRAVELING S	LOGGED	

TYPED NAME AND GRADE OF OFFICER OR OFFICIAL ON DUTY	SIGNATURE

DA FORM 1594, NOV 62   PREVIOUS EDITION OF THIS FORM IS OBSOLETE.   USAPPC V3.00

DAILY STAFF JOURNAL OR DUTY OFFICER'S LOG

For use of this form, see AR 220-15: the proponent agency
is Office of The Deputy Chief of Staff for Operations & Plans

PAGE NO.	NO. OF PAGES

ORGANIZATION OR INSTALLATION	LOCATION	PERIOD COVERED			
2/197 FA (MP)	BAQUBAH POLICE STATION, IRAQ	FROM		TO	
		HOUR 2400	DATE 20 APR 04	HOUR	DATE 20 APR 04

ITEM NO.	TIME IN	TIME OUT	INCIDENTS, MESSAGES, ORDERS, ETC.	ACTION TAKEN	INL
1	2359	0000	JOURNAL OPENED	LOGGED	
2	0814	0814	POSSIBLE IED @ MC 672319, FRESHLY DUG HOLE W/ CONCRETE SLAB PLACED ON TOP	LOGGED	
3	0815	1130	POSSIBLE IED @ MC 64233175, ROCKET W/ WIRES PROTRUDING, IRAQI QRF AND EOD EN ROUTE	LOGGED	
4	1038	1038	IED @ MC 662339 IS CLEARED, WASN'T AN IED	LOGGED	
5	1039	1039	POSSIBLE IED @ MC 641308, IRAQI QRF ON SITE	LOGGED	
6	1049	1049	1 AK-47 TEST FIRE	LOGGED	
7	1542	1544	WHITE VAN SPOTTED BY SCHOOL TO WEST OF STATION. TWO OCCUPANTS. SEEMED TO WANT	------------	
-----	------	------	TO UNLOAD BUT INSTEAD DROVE AWAY.	JOC NOTIFIED	
8	1555	1555	REPORT KIDS PLAYING IN FIELD N/E OF PD ONE MAN CAME PLACED 2-5 GAL. PAILS KIDS RAN AWAY	------------	
-----	-------	------	MAN LEFT DOWN ALLEY NEXT TO FIELD, MAN DRESSED IN BLACK PANTS, WHITE SHIRT	JOC NOTIFIED	
9	1941	1943	THREE PEOPLE BY A WHITE CAR, TALKING/STANDING BEHIND THE MOSQUE FOR LAST 15 MINS	JOC NOTIFIED	

TYPED NAME AND GRADE OF OFFICER OR OFFICIAL ON DUTY	SIGNATURE

DA FORM 1594, NOV 62   PREVIOUS EDITION OF THIS FORM IS OBSOLETE.   USAPPC V3.00

More by Baqubah Press

Philosophical Poetry and Pictures

Philosophical Poetry in the vein of Ludwig Wittgenstein. Find the meaning to life in your own imagination.

The Painter & The Writer

w/ Bob Farrell

This work is poetry born from paintings by Bob Farrell. Paintings were sent to Aaron and an original poem was created by viewing each piece separately and in its own world in the context of the painting and the surrounding image area. This book also showcases paintings by Bob Farrell.

The Demons of Purgonia

A Sci-Fi thriller about the true nature of humans. We are after all, natural machines.